# KID, YOU SING
# MY SONGS

Also by Lois Wyse

# Kid, you sing my songs

## of Love and Loss and Hope

### Lois Wyse

Illustrated by Lilla Rogers

Crown Publishers, Inc., New York

Grateful acknowledgment is made to *Good Housekeeping*
magazine for permission to reprint the following excerpts,
which were previously published in slightly different form:
"Sometimes the Music Doesn't Stop, It Just Gets Very Faint,"
"Troubled Waters," "A Little Night Music," "The Six-Acre
Husband," "The Charity Dance," "Divorce Advertising Style,"
"Dating Revisited, or How I Became My Daughter's Daughter,"
"Widow's Weeds," and "The Next Chapter."

Published by Crown Publishers, Inc., 201 East 50th Street,
New York, New York 10022. Member of the Crown Publishing Group.

CROWN is a trademark of Crown Publishers, Inc.
Manufactured in the United States of America

Library of Congress Cataloging-in-Publication Data

Wyse, Lois.
Kid, you sing my songs of love and loss and hope—/Lois Wyse.—1st ed.
p.   cm.
1. Wyse, Lois—Biography—Marriage.   2. Humorists, American—20th
century—Biography—Marriage.   3. Marriage—Humor.   I. Title.
PS3573.Y747469   1991
818'.6409—dc20

[B]                                                                 90-2403

CIP

ISBN 0-517-57705-4
10   9   8   7   6   5   4   3   2   1
First Edition

For the loves
that make
my heart sing

# CONTENTS

# INTRODUCTION

*L*ove and marriage are back in style.

No one knows just when or how it happened.

Was it the need to connect in a disconnected world? Could it have been the loud ticking of the biological clock? Or was it all prompted by the need to stay home and amortize the outrageous cost of a satellite dish?

Whatever the reason, old-fashioned hand-holding and kissing, wedding cakes and honeymoons, showers and babies are all making a big comeback.

Of course, there are some of us who thought that stuff was always in style.

Some of us learned early on that there is no facelift that works better than love, that nothing clears the sinuses better than a kiss, and that there is no pension plan to compare with the prospect of spending your years with someone who promises to love, honor, and cherish you.

However, while we may all aspire to love, few of us wake up one morning and take an elevator to love. So we spend a lot of our walking around time looking for love because love—good, strong love—takes bravery and a daring spirit, and not many are brave enough or daring enough to make lifetime commitments without investigating options. So, before we are able to settle into the comfort zone of a love, we dip into and discard relationships.

Yet even after all the wandering and wondering, even after

the stardust settles, many of us survey the results and wonder how it all happened this particular way.

"Why did you marry me?" a wife asked her husband on their second wedding anniversary. "After all," she reminded him, "we weren't exactly kids, and in this day of men marrying women young enough to be their daughters, I am old enough to be your wife."

He looked up and answered quietly, "I married you for three reasons.

"First, you didn't have a dog, so I knew you'd never send me out on a cold winter night.

"Second, you always made real coffee."

Now he paused and looked a look that held the memories of old losses and new paths. "The third reason is easy," he said. "Kid, you sing my songs."

You've probably guessed. I was the wife who asked the question. I was the wife who sang his songs. I couldn't carry a tune, but I sang his songs.

And I listened. To him and to everyone else who sang a song of love.

And this is a little book about some of the songs I heard.

Some are sweet.

Some are not.

But that's life.

That's love.

And who ever said that love always comes in a perfect gift-wrapped package?

# ...And How Did
# You Two Meet?

or years I watched him work magic just by waiting for the right time to ask The Question. He'd wait for that particular lull in the conversation, the turning point when it becomes either a ho-hum or a ho-ho evening, and then with a certain diffidence he'd ask The Question, sometimes of men, but more often of women.

Dinner parties were his favorite place to ask, preferably a party where the soufflé had fallen and the conversation had never had a chance to rise. At just the proper moment, he would give that I'm-going-to-do-it look, and I'd know he was about to charm the room and save the night.

Now I've made it a standard in my conversational repertoire, too. So be forewarned. At some point I'll ask...

*...and how did you two meet?*

I've asked absolute strangers and best friends. I've asked when standing in line at the movies and while sitting on buses. I've asked as I've waited for new soles and filets of sole.

I've heard sweet stories and sad ones, stories full of surprises and some so predictable I wondered why I asked. But what's wonderful is that there *are* stories, that there is love, and no one knows just when it's going to come along.

Kathy met Henry at the ballet. She thought he was married, and he thought she was cute.

She was wrong.

He was right.

When he asked what she did, she was so offended by the presumption of this "married" man that she answered icily, "I'm a brain surgeon."

He nodded. "I'm an investigative reporter."

Two days later when he called her at the ad agency where she worked, she couldn't believe he'd found her.

"I told you I'm an investigative reporter," he explained patiently. "Now will you go out with me?"

They went together—and separately—for a few years. At one back-together-again time he asked her to marry him. "Why are you asking me?" she wondered.

"Because I always thought you were cute; besides, you'll never meet anybody who's better for you than I am."

Who can say no to a man of reasons?

Cindy was moving into a new condo, her first home away from home. Her mother came to help unpack and oversee. As the two were getting the kitchen in order, Cindy looked out the window and saw her neighbor walking to the swimming pool.

"Hmmmm," Cindy mused, "we certainly could use some help here, and that fellow in the next apartment looks big and strong. I wonder if he's married."

He wasn't then.

He is now.

To Cindy.

What man can fail to fall for the girl next door?

Barbara was a dental hygienist when she met Bob.

Cute guy, bad gums.

So Barbara did what she had to: she cleaned his teeth four times a year.

And while he rinsed, she waited out the old wife, the new girl-friends and the usual obstacles.

In the end, of course, he married her.

How do you turn down the woman who brightens your smile?


So how did I meet Lee, the man who always asked others how they met?

By professional accident.

In the 1970s I was writing poetry books about what I thought love was; I wrote out of dreams and hopes, and they seem to have matched a lot of other people's dreams and hopes because they became fairly popular.

Then one day I received a telephone call from Peggy Lee's manager. It seems she was one of the people who read what I wrote.

Miss Lee was scheduled to open at the Waldorf in New York, and she wanted to include some of my poems in her act. The manager wondered what I wanted for the rights.

I couldn't believe this was happening.

Peggy Lee, perfect Peggy Lee with her faultless taste and matchless talent, wanted to read my stuff! I could scarcely get the words out. "All I want is a ringside table opening night, and she can use my material forever."

It was, as they say, an offer she couldn't refuse.

So on opening night there I was at ringside. Peggy Lee sang her first number, did a couple of other songs, and then she quoted several Carl Sandburg poems.

I figured that was it.

She's using Sandburg, not me.

Who could blame her? What would you take? One of the most famous, honored American poets or a girl from Cleveland?

15

Don't be disappointed, I told me. You're in this fancy room at the Waldorf, so relax. Have a good time. Some people never get this far. I took my advice, settled back and just listened.

Oh, that Peggy Lee was good. So good.

And then, then just when I was into her music and out of my thoughts, she did it.

Out of the blue, in the middle of the show, she recited two of my poems.

... and how did you two meet?

Forget Poet's Corner.

At that moment I was in Poet's Heaven, and it was live at the Waldorf, a lot better than dead in Westminster Abbey.

At the end of her act, Peggy Lee acknowledged my presence and invited me to stand. I did, and when I sat down, I saw that a man had come to our table. He was all charm and smiles. He was also one of the best-looking men I'd ever seen in my life, and he said, "My name is Lee Guber. I like your work very much."

Now, who wouldn't love a man with that kind of taste?

# I LOVE YOU
# BETTER NOW

Before I was in love with you,
I was in love with love.
Oh, what a lovely love
Of cloudless climes and starry skies
With a man that never was.

    This was me,
    The me who lived with girly girl beliefs
    Until she lived with you,
    And little by little,
    Slice by slice,
    Like the layers of wallpaper
    In a hundred-year-old house,
    You stripped the pink dreams down.

Off with the cabbage roses,
Down with the merry maids.

Backward turns the clock.

Where does reality begin?
When did you peel the last old pattern
And find there really was a woman
Under such a lot of girl?

# ACCIDENTAL LOVE

At seventy-nine Mervin hadn't expected it to happen.
Death maybe.
Arthritis for sure.
But love?
Unbelievable.
Still, it had happened.

The nice thing was that it was one of those kinds of loves your kids could look at from five hundred miles away—which was where they lived these days—and say, "Good for you, Pop."

Well, why shouldn't they be happy for him?

Evelyn was a lovely lady. Marjorie herself had said so. They'd all met in Florida one winter when they were staying at the same hotel. He was there with Marjorie, and Evelyn was with Herb. That's how it is when you grow old with your first marriage. You work a little. Finally you retire, and then you play a little.

Ten years ago it was that the four of them met; two older

couples trying to cope with retirement and grown kids and grandchildren and a few new aches and pains.

Then five years ago they'd heard that Herb had died. Not long afterward Marjorie became ill, and for two years Mervin hovered as her nurse-companion while she cheated death—and was cheated on life—because their lifestyle was never the same. Bedridden and cheerless, Marjorie became another person. She didn't simply accept Merv's time and attention; she demanded it, and by the time she died, he was too weary of his sad life to look for a new one.

Then, one year ago, when the last of his children moved away, Merv decided that he needed a woman in his life. So he called Evelyn. She lived a few towns away, but still he had the car and the yen to drive it, so it was all right.

Every Friday night he got into his Buick and drove to Evelyn's house. He'd take her to dinner, take her home and then go to a nice motel near her house.

But now, after a year of this courtship, Merv decided they ought to have a little adventure in their lives. Not Florida, he reasoned. Why visit old memories? Better to make new ones. He checked the Auto Club and found a nice old-fashioned bed-and-breakfast place just two hours from her house.

Pleased as punch, Merv told Evelyn he had a surprise for her. Evelyn smiled. Wouldn't it be fun to have a little romance just when everyone thought the fires had died?

They'd gone only twenty-seven miles when the car veered off the road and into a ditch. Merv screamed, "Evelyn, are you all right?"

"Yeeees," was the tremulous answer.

For an hour Merv kept running his fingers through his thinning hair. How had this happened? Two simultaneous blowouts —never happens—the garage man said. But the paramedics appeared, and they insisted on taking Evelyn and Merv to the local hospital.

"We're all right," Merv insisted.

"Let's be sure," Evelyn said in a small voice.

So Herb let the ambulance take them to the nearest hospital, and sadly he called and canceled their reservations.

At the hospital, Evelyn said to Merv as she went in for X rays, "You'd best call my daughter."

Merv nodded, but his knees wouldn't carry him to the telephone down the hall. How do you call a daughter and tell her that her mother, on her way to a vacation, was just sidetracked by an accident and was now in a hospital?

"Shall I call for you?" the nurse asked in that solicitous tone that meant the well-starched lady didn't think he had the strength or the courage to phone.

"No." He stood up and was swept down the hall by a surge of adrenaline.

Evelyn's daughter arrived and asked to see the doctor. "My mother is a very old woman—" she began, and then she saw the hurt in Merv's eyes. Did he think that she was judging him and holding him responsible for her mother's welfare?

"Perhaps we should talk alone," Evelyn's daughter said softly.

Merv began to protest, and then he realized that there might be something in Evelyn's medical history she'd never want him to know. Suddenly he felt that he was in a room where he had no right to be. "I'll leave," he offered.

Alone together, Evelyn's daughter turned to the doctor. "Tell me truthfully, will my mother be all right?"

"Your mother will be fine. I'd suggest a few days here for observation, and then she can be on her way again," the doctor said with that practiced medical calm.

Evelyn's daughter leaned back and smiled with relief. "Wow, the things you go through when your mother is dating," she laughed.

"But your mother," the doctor interjected, "is in remarkable health for a woman seventy-nine years of age."

Now her daughter laughed out loud. "Seventy-nine?"

"Amazing condition," the doctor said, stepping up his analysis.

"But, Doctor," she protested further, "my mother's not seventy-nine."

"Not seventy-nine?"

"No, she's ninety-one. But that shows you how remarkable she really is. She's been in an automobile accident, comes to a hospital—and still she remembers to lie about her age. Dear Merv will never know how we women lie for love."

# WANTED: ONE RIGHT MAN

Josie is getting married this month, and while that may not surprise you, it certainly does surprise Josie. It's not that Josie isn't smart, cute and employed. She is all three.

But she is also over thirty (thirty-one to be exact), and if you have been reading the magazines, you know that women over thirty have about as much chance of meeting and marrying a nice, red-blooded, two-fisted male as they do of becoming paratroopers.

In other words, it's possible but unlikely.

Josie was not the only one who was beginning to despair of her chances.

Her whole family was concerned.

Each night Josie came home from work, saw the red light blinking on her telephone answering machine, flipped the switch and heard her grandfather's voice: "So, Josie, you found your Mr. Right today?"

Life finally got to the point where Josie didn't even turn on the answering machine, and as anyone knows you have to be pretty desperate not to do that.

One night, however, Josie went to her mother's home for dinner. Her grandfather was there. "Josie, I been thinking," Grandpa said. "You haven't met Mr. Right yet, and I have a little money. There's a computer dating service I saw advertised. You get to see pictures, and then you go to nice parties with speakers, brunches in good restaurants. You join this, I'll pay for one year. Maybe Mr. Right will join, too."

Josie's year was almost up when she saw Steve's picture. Steve remembers reading what Josie wrote about herself and thinking she was his kind of woman. When he saw her picture, he hoped that was what she really looked like.

And so they met.

And yes, they're getting married.

"It may not be the usual way to meet someone," Josie says, "but it worked. And the best part is that when I come home at night, and the light is flashing on my answering machine, it's never my grandfather; it's Steve."

Another thirty-plus I know ran an ad in a magazine in the city where she lives. The headline was, BLOND MARY TYLER MOORE.

Did it work?

The ad worked, but the marriage didn't. The blond MTM got forty responses and picked a scientist. It seems scientists don't have a lot of time to go out and meet girls. Now our blond friend is alone once more, but she's cooling her heels—and her pen—before she writes another ad.

The women in my office were talking the other day about the gloomy prospects predicted for them.

Said Sharon: "I'm tired of worrying about dates. I love football, and if there's no man around, I'd just as soon stay home and watch a good football game all by myself."

Stacy took out a pencil and paper. "I'm writing your ad now," she said. "There isn't a man in the world who won't want a woman who turns *on* the game."

We'll see.

# THE EYE OF THE BEHOLDER

F-a-t.

It is the ugliest three-letter word in a woman's lexicon. The very idea that it might describe her sends a female of any age into depression, turns a one-time charmer into a nagging harridan and threatens her with loss of self-respect and dignity.

Still, f-a-t was the only way to describe Beth Jo.

She wasn't a fatty-come-lately. No, she'd been sent to Camp Chubby as a child, had drunk a variety of meal-in-a-shake fad diets, nibbled lettuce leaves while friends OD'd on chocolate frenzies—but nothing worked.

Beth Jo remained f-a-t.

The Fat Doctor said it was an emotional problem. The psychiatrist said it was a confusion between punishment and reward. And her mother, a candidate for anorexia, said she couldn't understand how she had ended up with the Incredible Hulk for a daughter.

By the time Beth Jo was ready for college, she'd had it with all of the family and professional advice. Since I seem to be born f-a-t, she told herself, I might as well enjoy it.

So, from the day she left for school she ate everything she wanted to eat. Amazingly she didn't gain weight, and she didn't lose weight. She ate her way through four years of college, and after graduation went out and got herself a job with a large cosmetics company with worldwide offices.

Despite her fat body, Beth Jo was no fat head. She was a numbers whiz who found herself much in demand from nine to five. It was from five to nine that no one called.

So Beth Jo created her own world, went out with her women friends, attended concerts and theater, tried all the new restaurants, and found she could afford to live any way she wanted because her salary kept increasing.

Within a year Beth Jo was doing complicated financial analyses for the company, making money where no one thought it was possible and dealing with exchange rates in a highly complex work situation. "There's a problem in Milan," her boss said one day. "Beth Jo, see how fast you can straighten out those lira people and get them to think dollars. Get on a plane to Milan, will you?"

Beth Jo nodded as she sugared her coffee and ate another jelly doughnut.

Because she was a visiting American from the home office, the head of the Milan group took her to dinner with his wife. Halfway through dinner they were joined by the young assistant in the office. Beth Jo took one look at him and stopped her fork in midair. The Italian assistant was straight and lean and dark and as perfect as a six-page spread in *GQ*.

Beth Jo was struck dumb.

Just one look, and she was crazy in love. Smitten. Mad about the boy. She wanted to speak, but no words came. Petrified and panic-stricken, she began eating as fast as she could so she wouldn't be able to speak—and say the wrong words.

During dinner the assistant spoke a great deal, ate sparingly and—having been told of the importance of Beth Jo's position —after dinner followed his boss's suggestion and walked Beth Jo around the city before escorting her back to her hotel.

He thought her silence was a sign of shyness and breeding.

Two months later the Italian assistant came to the States. Now Beth Jo was able to find just the words she needed because her job was to explain the new accounting system. He rubbed his eyes. Under the mounds of fat was a woman who knew how to think lean and mean.

Some months later he came back to the United States. Soon he was returning each month. Most of us would not call their business meetings a romance. But unsophisticated Beth Jo could—and did.

"If you're really interested in this young man, you'll prove it to him and lose weight," her mother advised.

"Mmmm," Beth Jo answered, brushing the croissant crumbs from her lips.

"He'll never marry you," her engaged sister warned. "He's just letting you help him. You're nothing but a way to the top."

"Probably," Beth Jo agreed as she hung up the phone, went to the freezer and dug into the pint of Ben & Jerry's newest frozen chocolate masterpiece.

It was two years after they met that Beth Jo confessed to him —over gnocchi in Milan—that she loved him and wanted him to marry her.

He played with his food and explained that romance was Italian but marriage wasn't.

Beth Jo shrugged and ordered biscuit tortoni.

In June Beth Jo was telexed some news. The father of her beloved had died. Beth Jo wrote a long, understanding letter, and one week later, with no advance notice, her Italian appeared in the office.

"Beth Jo," he said, "let's go to lunch."

Beth Jo frowned. He must be in a terrible state to be here so soon after his father's death. She sighed. She knew he either wanted advice on how to handle his father's estate or he had an office emergency.

She was wrong. Over pasta primavera he did the one thing she never expected him to do. He asked her to marry him.

Beth Jo burst into tears and never put a fork in her food.

It is two years now since they were married.

During that time Beth Jo has lost what she now calls "my

baby fat." Love has slimmed her to a sylphlike body. She is, as they say, a looker.

"How did you know there was such a good-looking woman under that fat?" the head of the Milan office asked. "How did you know marriage would change her so?"

"She hasn't changed," Beth Jo's new husband replied. "I knew all about her when I asked her to marry me. I went to the States when my father died because suddenly I realized that nothing is forever. Not me. Not my father. But my father goes on so long as I love, marry and have children. Then I thought—who? Who is there for me to love? The skinny little models? The brainless girls? No. I want a woman to be wife to me, mother to my children. I thought of Beth Jo. And I thought, with all my heart,

she is the most beautiful woman I know. Her beauty shines through. You think beauty takes a certain shape? I don't think so. Now that Beth Jo has resculptured her body, you think she is different. But she is as sweet and loving and warm as she was that day she was brave enough to say she loved me. You, dear friend, are the one who's changed."

# SINGLE:
# A FEW THOUGHTS
# ON BEING

Men are like real estate.
The best ones are never on the market.


The unmarried woman's greeting card:
Whatever happened to all the cute, interesting single men we should be dating?
They're dating each other.


Line from a notebook:
Happiness is making the most of what you have, and riches is making the most of what you've got.


She is old enough to date and young enough to discard imperfect men with perfect reasoning.

*Scene: Aerobics class at the gym.*
*Characters: Two single women.*

SW 1: What's your idea of the perfect man?

SW 2: He should have a great sense of humor. Also he should be a very good kisser. And that's it.

SW 1: Just a sense of humor and a good kisser? That's all?

SW 2: Look, honey, I've got a gym for exercise.

I met a divorced woman who was angry because widows got all the sympathy.

I met a widow who was angry because divorcées got all the money.

I met a wife who was angry because married women don't get any sympathy *or* money.

If you love someone, you don't need any reasons.
If you *don't* love someone, you need 135 reasons.

WINNING AND LOSING THE LOVE GAME:
HIS AND HER VIEWS

SHE: You win some and you lose some—but you have to dress for both.

HE: You win some and you lose some—but nobody believes either story anyway.

# AND ON THE
# EIGHTH DAY . . .

ony was the one child in the family his parents never could understand. The two girls? Easy. One became a housewife (a traditionalist like her mom) and the other became a hotshot career lady (a new person like her contemporaries). Mama and Papa had no trouble with either of those girls.

But Tony?

Forget it.

Tony never worked seriously at anything. Part-time here for a few dollars, full-time there for a few weeks. He didn't like work, so why should he be bothered? Instead, long after his contemporaries had left their hippie lives, Tony was still dropping out. He floated around the world, picked up a job here or there and managed to stay warm and dry. At least no one in the family heard otherwise.

And then one day his sister Gerry got the call.

"Hi, Gerry. This is Tony."

It had been so long, and her brother was so far from her everyday thinking, that she immediately answered, "Tony who?"

"Tony, your brother. That's who."

"What's wrong?" she asked.

Tony laughed. He knew the family couldn't exactly think the best of anything if he called. Indeed the last time she'd seen Tony was at their mother's funeral three years earlier. "Nothing's wrong," he assured her, "but I need some help. My apart-

ment is going co-op, and I can get a lot of money for it if I buy it now and then sell it in a few months. Want to invest and be my partner?"

Gerry, the career sister, said, "Sure. But let's see each other."

Gerry called Penny, the housewife sister, and she called her father. They had dinner at Penny's house, and Papa asked the same old question: "So? You have a job yet?"

"Not exactly," Tony answered, "but I have to be in the city for a while until my apartment goes co-op."

"Will you work?" Penny wondered aloud.

"When I have to," Tony answered in his familiar cavalier way.


It was two weeks later that Gerry was having dinner with one of her oldest friends, Veronica, a corporate strategist. "I am in a real jam," Veronica admitted.

Gerry smiled. She was accustomed to Veronica's jams. It could be something as major as too little time for a project or something as minor as new pantyhose. But this time she really was in a jam. Veronica had bought a new house, had to go out of town and didn't have anyone to do the punch list, to go over those finishing items that mean a house is really done, and you can pay the contractor the final payment.

Just like that Gerry had an idea. "I'll get my brother."

"I didn't even know you had a brother."

"Sometimes I don't. But he has to be in town for a while, so I'm sure he'd be glad to do this for you. He's been a sailor. He knows his way on ships, so he must know how to deal with carpenters and plumbers and painters."

And he did.

In fact, Tony did such a good job that Veronica called Gerry

when she returned from her trip and said, "Your brother is fabulous."

"Nice maybe," Gerry admitted grudgingly, "but no one has ever called my brother fabulous."

"He is. Believe me," Veronica said. "He's so good I'm going to send him to my friend Prudence, who lives in the village. She's a lawyer who's been buying property, and she needs somebody to do some work in her house and work on her other houses."

"Good luck," Gerry said. What had she started?

When Tony walked into Prudence's house, he took one look at Prudence and fell in love. Tony, age forty-six, never married and never employed, had fallen in love at first sight with a major overachiever, a woman who'd put herself through law school, scrambled her way through prestigious law firms, hoarded her pennies and was now preparing for her old age by buying houses.

"I love you," Tony declared.

"First fix the molding," Prudence the pragmatist instructed.

So Tony went to work that morning and managed to stretch a two-hour job into an eight-hour job. By five he still wasn't finished.

When Prudence came home, she was a bit agitated. "You're not finished, and I'm having a dinner party," she said testily.

"Good, I'll stay for the party," he offered.

"No." Prudence was adamant. "You cannot come to my party." What was she to do? Say to her influential guests, "Here's the plasterer. He couldn't finish the job, so he stayed for dinner"?

"I can't come to the party? Okay," Tony shrugged, "but I won't leave you. I'll wait in the bathtub until they leave."

"You're crazy," Prudence said.

"I know," Tony agreed, "crazy in love."

Prudence giggled. There were worse things in life than a man in your bathtub.

A week later Veronica called Gerry. "Listen," she said, "I see all the symptoms. My friend Prudence is falling in love with your brother, and your brother has no visible means of support. My friend Prudence cannot love anyone who doesn't accomplish something. Think about it. It's going to be an absolute disaster on both sides. We have to do something."

Gerry called Tony. "What's going on?"

"I'm in love," he sighed.

"So I understand," she replied crisply. "This requires some conversation."

They met in a Chinese restaurant, and Tony babbled on and on about his love.

When the fortune cookies arrived, Gerry put her hand on the first one. "I'll tell you what yours says," she said, looking at her brother. Then, without opening the cookie, she said in a sing-song voice as if she were reading from the little paper inside the cookie, "You will be a contractor. You will do very well. You will be able to get married."

"I get the picture," her brother answered. His apartment sold that week, and he saw a lot of money in hand for the first time in his life. He paid Gerry for her share of the investment, and he called Prudence. "I've got a case upstate," she told him. "I'm on my way now. I'll be back in a week, but I have good news. I bought another building, and I can give it to you for renovation. We have to meet in eight days with the new management group."

"Okay," he agreed, but there was uncertainty in his tone. He put the phone down, and instead of running out to buy a suit and tie, Tony hurried down to the docks, bought a boat and set sail for the tieless, briefcaseless easy life he'd been waiting to afford.

For seven days he let the wind lead him, and then on the eighth day he felt disquiet. That was when he knew that he had a decision to make. He truly loved Prudence. He truly loved the sea. Which was it to be? But even as he was weighing his choices, he sensed the answer.

The sea would be there forever.

Prudence would not.

So, on the ninth day, Tony turned sail and went back to port.

"Gerry," he announced, "I'm back, and Prudence and I are getting married."

"Think you can handle it at forty-six? I mean never having been married before—"

"I think so," he said solemnly. "Now I'm going to tell Dad."

At eighty-six, Tony's father didn't even have to meet Prudence to give his blessing. "I should tell you, Dad, that Prudence and I are not of the same religion—"

"Of course. She works and you don't," his father retorted.

"You know what I mean, Dad. So I want to ask something. Would it bother you if I got married in her church? It's important to her mother."

"Bother me?" His father shrugged. "Listen, you want to get married, I'll walk you down the aisle. I'll push you toward the altar. I'll name a room. Just go and do it."

And so Tony, the seafaring brother with no work habits, married Prudence, the woman of responsibility.

On the first anniversary of Tony and Prudence's marriage, Veronica and Gerry, the two matchmakers, went to lunch.

"What does she say?" Gerry asked.

"Prudence is the happiest woman in town," Veronica announced.

"Why not?" Gerry asked. "He made a fortune cookie prediction come true. Do you know he now has a huge contracting business and fifty-one employees? Do you realize, Veronica, that because of the love of one woman there are fifty-one people who now have terrific jobs? You see, love can make anything happen."

"Provided there are two women in the background like us," Veronica announced as she raised her glass.

# THE
# FRONT LINES

Love is not as easy as it used to be. Just ask my friend Peppy.

When she meets a new man, she has a mental checklist:

Is he married?

Is he gay?

Does he have a job?

If he passes on those points, then the big question:

Is he healthy?

"It's getting more and more difficult to meet good eligibles,"

Peppy admits, "although I'm not even sure what constitutes an eligible male any longer.

"Eligible used to mean taller and older, but there are a lot of nice, short, younger men. That's why I decided to go out with a younger man a couple of weeks ago. That's the trendy thing, isn't it? I mean all the big stars are doing it, so it must make you feel good. Well, I accepted a date with this twenty-three-year-old fellow, and even though there's only a ten-year difference in our ages, he treated me like his mother, and to tell you the truth, I didn't know whether to kiss him or burp him.

"Then this week a friend introduced me to an artist. Now that intrigued me. An artist! A live artist! I could just see myself going with an artist to all the interesting galleries. Oh, with a man like that you'd always have something to discuss. Besides, his friends would be Really Smart People. I could hardly wait for the night of our date. We had an incredible time, the best time I've had in years. At dinner we talked together about politics and art and music, and I thought he was very good-looking, nice, interesting. Then came the moment of truth. Did I want to see his work? How could I say no? Of course I wanted to see his work, so he took me to his studio. And I just stood there. I hated his work. I loved his looks, but I hated his work. I didn't want to offend him, so I just shook my head in disbelief. How could such a good guy paint such terrible stuff? I'm so disappointed. His art is obviously what he's really like, and the more I think about that, the more I hate his work.

"You know," she continued, "you get so frustrated meeting the wrong men that the only thing to do is to work out. I've decided to take all this physical energy that could go into making a man happy and go back to running. I was up at five A.M. today running around the park, and what do you know? A

fabulous-looking man was tooting his horn and waving at me. I waved back, and as he drove on, I saw his license plate. It said LOVE YA. I had to run fast from that. How can you explain to a man in a Porsche that you're not interested in men who have a relationship with their license plates?"

# WHAT I DID
# FOR LOVE

When they boarded the train outside Paris, passengers could not fail to notice them.

They were scrubbed and pretty and well dressed, two young women of an uncertain age in the age of uncertainty, those up-and-down years between World War I and World War II.

Like two dutiful schoolchildren, although they were several years past school age, they read their books as the train rocked along, station after station.

Finally Yvette sighed and yawned. This was getting pretty boring. "We still have an hour," she said fretfully.

"I know," her friend answered.

"I'm hungry," Yvette announced. "Let's find the diner."

And so the two, arm-locked in that old-fashioned best chum style, made their way precariously through the swaying cars.

They squeezed through the doors, giggled as they tried to keep their balance by moving quickly down the aisles and then —then she saw him. He was scrunched with another boy in a single backseat (anything to save a franc). The two boys were obviously very tall because their knees were touching their chins.

Yvette dropped her arm from her friend's waist and stared in wonder at the most handsome young man she'd ever seen. His eyes met hers, and she knew she was his forever.

Never mind that a boyfriend of six years was waiting in her town to take her to the ball the next night.

Never mind that she had promised to marry that boy.

All she knew was that this was today, now was the moment, and she was looking at a boy with bony knees whose blue eyes made her heart stop.

Yvette took one step forward, tripped over the young man's feet and went sprawling on the floor of the car.

He stumbled from his two-for-one seat and rushed to help her to her feet. "Let me escort you back to your seat," he offered gallantly.

She murmured yes (ohhhh, those blue eyes), and with his arm supporting her, this woman who only minutes before had been robust was suddenly weak and clinging as she limped on his arm from car to car.

By the time she reached her seat, he had asked her to the ball the next night.

Of course the story has a happy ending.

The young couple married, raised a wonderful family, and lived a long and happy life together until his death a few years ago.

Now, embraced by the sweetness of memory and the love of her children, Yvette thinks back often to the early days. But as she retold the story one day and came to the part about tripping, she stopped.

"I must tell you the truth," she said soberly to her daughters.

"You know the way Papa always told the story? He said I'd tripped. It's not true. I didn't trip. I just decided to fall at his feet. My heart told me he'd be the kind of boy who'd take care of me, and I thought—why not find out right away and save a lot of time later on?"

"But why didn't you admit the truth after all those years?" a daughter asked.

Mama put her hands up. "And spoil Papa's story? Never."

# SINGULAR PLEASURES

They have been friends all their lives, these two women, and now they have decided to celebrate that day of great hopes—their fortieth birthday—together. One is married, one is not. Still, they want no men, no big party, no noisemakers, no cakes with candles.

Instead the two will treat themselves to dinner at the city's fanciest restaurant. I am warmed by the thought, but still I wonder what would dear Aunt Edna have thought of that?

My Aunt Edna was what we used to call a "spinster," the unmarried daughter who lived at home with her mother in a time when "nice girls" didn't leave home until they married.

And Aunt Edna never married.

She dreamed her dreams, I am sure, but she never shared them. Still, she never made me feel sorry for her; instead she took both pride and joy in my life and later extended that affectionate care to my children.

Aunt Edna had friends, women who were, for the most part, just like Aunt Edna—educated and traveled teachers, librarians, secretaries.

They rejoiced in one another's nieces and nephews, the commencements and confirmations, later the graduations and engagements, and each year Aunt Edna and her friends took a trip—but rarely did any two of the friends go together.

Did they need that time apart from their regular friendship, a vacation from their endless stories of family, in order to replenish the library of their lives?

Were they trying to live new stories to tell the old friends?

I never really knew. And I was too shy to ask.

And now, a generation later, two women will proudly announce that they are forty, and they will go out and spend a hundred dollars on a dinner for themselves. In Aunt Edna's day, friendships ended when marriages began.

Married women did not share any part of their lives with the unmarried.

And certainly a married woman did not go out on the town with an unmarried friend.

Two women alone in a fancy restaurant?

What would the neighbors say?

How lucky that today we do not let marriage or nonmarriage interrupt the warmth of our shared history, shared affection, shared memories and shared dreams.

I doubt if anyone knew when Aunt Edna celebrated her fortieth birthday.

Ladies of all ages never revealed any ages.

I know only that when my dear Aunt Edna was going to have her eightieth birthday, I told her that I wanted to give a luncheon for her and invite her friends, and I asked her to send

40

me the names and addresses of those long-ago librarians and teachers and secretaries.

At the bottom of the list Aunt Edna appended this note: "Lois dear, I appreciate your having this party, but please—when you send invitations—do not mention which birthday this is. Some of the girls don't know how old I am."

And at the party Aunt Edna blew out three candles—for past, present and future—and just before she blew them out, one friend asked, "How old are you, Edna?"

Aunt Edna looked at me with her watery blue eyes and said quietly, "Well, Lois thinks I'm three."

# CONFESSIONS OF A HOME WRECKER

So take a look at me. I'm not thin. I'm not gorgeous. I'm not rich. I don't even have a high school diploma. Is this the face and the body of a home wrecker, I ask you? Well, the answer is yes. His ex calls me a home wrecker, and to her I am. But not to him. To him I'm a homemaker.

"Let me take it from the top. He was a fancy executive, and I was a cocktail waitress. See? Already you're on her side. But it wasn't how you think. The rich wife was out spending his money while I was out making mine. My first husband walked when my two kids were aged one and two. I don't blame him. I would've walked if I could. The house was a mess. We couldn't even afford a sitter. All I did was take care of two kids. After he left I worked in a drive-in, took other kids in for working moth-

ers when I was at home—anything to make a buck and hold on to my babies.

"Finally...it was five years later, and I looked ten years older ...I got this good job as a cocktail waitress. The guys liked to pinch, but I had a rule: 'No dates.' I figured if a guy needed a bar after work, he must be some kind of married. You know, fully married, half married, or half-past married.

"I'll admit I noticed him right from the start because he was different. He was a real gentleman. He was always polite. Good tipper, too. We'd talk a little, not much. He showed me a picture of his kids, and I showed him a picture of mine. It was that kind of talk. Not sexy, sort of family. But then one day...he got me on a real bad day...it was two days before Christmas. He said, 'What are you doing with the kids for the holiday?' and I did my brave little single-mom bit, chin high, eyes bright. And then damned if, right in the middle of it all, I didn't cry my eyes out.

"He took me out for dinner that night.

"But you knew I'd get to that part, didn't you? Still, it's not how you think. I didn't want to go out again. But he begged me and begged me. It's not as if I hadn't always read Dear Abby. I knew the score. I knew dating the married guys was no-win for the other woman. But he kept saying he needed me, and he wanted to see me. Every time I'd say this was the end, and I was going to go, he'd plead, 'Don't go don't go don't go.' So I stayed.

"All he wanted was a wife to be at home.

"All she wanted was a husband to take her out, move her up.

"So we had a four-year secret affair followed by a two-year public divorce and a lifetime disgrace in the hometown. As soon as we got married, we moved to California.

"That was all twenty-three years ago, and today I guess you could say that we have the best marriage of any of our friends.

"Not bad for a home wrecker, huh?"

# THE STATE OF US

Why do we kiss when we part,
Then kiss as we meet?
Because the kiss reminds us
Where we are,
And lets us continue
Uninterrupted
The flow of life.

# BONJOUR, PAPA

The plane had reached its cruising altitude several hours earlier. The drinks had been poured and dinner served for the long flight from Paris to New York, and now the film flickered on.

Lucie half-watched. Ho hum. Another American movie with a bunch of American movie stars. She glanced at Paul, her ten-year-old son in the seat next to her. Certainly Paul didn't care about the film. He had two American comic books, but they sat at his feet unread, for Paul's real entertainment on this flight was his window seat. How he loved the window seat. In amusement Lucie shook her well-shaped head with the chicly cropped

43

black hair. Foolish child. He wanted the window seat when there was nothing to see. Not yet anyway, but he'd asked for that seat so that he could be the first to see New York. He would see New York and pass the view along to Mama.

Lucie rang the service bell. Perhaps a glass of wine and the images on the screen would work together to lull her to sleep.

She sipped slowly, her mind going back over the years to— when suddenly she saw him.

There. There on the screen she saw him.

"My God, Paul," she choked, "there's your Papa. Look. Up on the screen. It's your Papa."

"Papa?" the boy echoed in confusion. "Why is he up there?" the boy asked, looking toward the first-class section of the plane.

"Not up there. Not in a seat. Up there on the screen. In the movie. Your Papa," she said half to herself. "Who would think you'd see him before he ever saw you?"

"I thought Papa was in California," Paul murmured.

"That's where he lived when I met him," Lucie explained. "Papa was a movie actor. He went to Cannes for the film festival, and we met there."

"Why did he leave us, Mama?"

"His work was in America. He was not a Frenchman, and my son didn't need an American father. You are a Frenchman."

"But I always asked you why he never came to see us. I want my Papa," the boy cried. "Give me my Papa."

Lucie turned her back to her son just as she had turned her back on his father, Kevin. Now the memories rushed back. Their brief affair, the letters she'd returned unopened. She'd never told him of her pregnancy lest he seek the boy. But the boy was hers; she wanted a child, and he was able to give her one. Did

he also want a child? Lucie never knew. After all, she hadn't known him long enough or well enough to ask.

Now there was no need to ask.

Now there was a demand. Paul wanted Papa.

Lucie turned to her son.

Why not find him his Papa?

Yes, why not? This was the perfect time to find Papa. It was somewhat charming for an unmarried woman of the moment to have a baby, a small son—but this boy, this boy was going to be too big to explain to the new young lovers crowding her life.

It was not difficult to find Kevin. He was listed with the Screen Actors' Guild, and he flew to New York the very day he received the call from Lucie.

No, he had never married.

No, he had not forgotten that weekend.

And yes, yes he'd wondered why she had never written to him and why his letters were returned unopened. No, he did not take returned, unopened mail as a French signal of pregnancy, and he doubted that any other man would.

Still, there was no denying his son. The boy had the forelock of his forebears, Kevin's smile, but he was so—so French. "I wish I could take you to California," he said to his son and his mother. "Wouldn't you like to play tennis and—"

"Take him," Lucie said quickly. She'd known she'd say that the moment Kevin's image appeared on the screen. "The boy will enjoy living like an American," she said softly. Silently she assured herself that his soul was French.

Kevin took to fatherhood with all the instincts of an old-fashioned parent. He waded with Paul through the murky waters of the teen years, guided him past the temptations of his early adulthood, and when he reached his late twenties, Paul met a girl at the research center where he worked.

They went to live together in Southern California, and neither said a word about marriage. Instead they talked about surfing and sun and seas. Then one morning she turned to Paul and said, "I'm pregnant. What do you want me to do?"

"Whatever you want," he answered quickly.

"I want the child, but I know your history. I don't want to drag you kicking and screaming into marriage—"

"You won't," he told her firmly. "Marriage does not run in my family. My father has never married; my mother has never married. Why should I break the spell?"

"But the baby?"

"I think we can have a baby without a wedding ceremony."

The day Paul told Kevin about the baby, he thought his father looked a bit wistful. "You're not going to marry her?" he asked.

"Of course not." Paul smiled. "Papa, I'm a Frenchman. You're not even a Frenchman, and look at you. Many ladies over the years, but not a marriage. And the one you're with now—"

"I am going to marry her," Kevin said firmly although he hadn't known he would until he heard his son's words. "Nancy and I have been together two years, I've known her for twenty, and we're going to get married," he said as much to himself as to his son.

"Amazing." Paul turned to his father with a faint, embarrassed smile. "You're so American, Papa."

"No," his father responded, "I am caring. I'd hoped that after all these years with me, you would be as well. I care for Nancy deeply, and the moment you said you were not going to get married, I knew that I would. I don't want generations of chil-

dren with unmarried parents. I want stability and love. What does it matter if you give your child two playpens and an Alexander Calder mobile if you do not give him two parents and a stable life?"

The two couples were married a week later in a double ceremony.

Said Kevin, "It's enough that my son had an unmarried father. My grandson will have a married father and a married grandfather. It's—well, let's say it's American."

# ANNIVERSARY
# SONG

Someone asked me
To name the time
Our friendship stopped
And love began.

Oh, my darling,
That's the secret:
Our friendship
Never stopped.

# RAINY NIGHT LOVE

I t was a benefit, one of those formal-dress parties that is long on people but short on fun. Then, just as we were to leave the museum where the party was being held, the rains came.

The men in their formal dress went to find their cars or taxis, and we women stood huddled in the doorway, ready to run between raindrops as soon as our transportation arrived, for the narrow side street was jammed with automobiles and their impatient drivers.

And then a car stopped at the door, but no woman came forward. We looked around, and standing in the lobby—safe and dry—was a woman who'd been seated at our table. We peered into the night. "It's your husband's car," we called to her, mindful of the honking autos now lining up like planes on a runway.

She smiled benignly but did not move.

The chorus of horns grew louder. Still, she did not move.

Then the door of the car opened, and her husband came out, umbrella in hand.

He raised the umbrella, walked purposefully but calmly through the clutch of milling women directly to his wife, and took her arm.

Slowly, carefully avoiding the flooding curbs, he led her to the car as other drivers, unmindful of the rain, were rolling down their windows and roiling the night with their epithets.

Still unhurried by the weather and unruffled by the other motorists, he escorted her to the car under his umbrella. He opened her door, settled her in the front seat, and then—to the

consternation of the people in the cars behind his—he did not go to his side of the car.

Instead he walked back toward the lobby.

Now a clutch of incensed drivers spilled from their cars and shouted angrily at his retreating figure.

But he paid no attention. He was a man with a mission.

With a smile and a bow, he stepped into the lobby and deposited the umbrella he had borrowed from the checkroom.

And, gracefully as a ballroom dancer, he executed a small turn and strolled leisurely through the raindrops to his car.

When he reached his car, he bowed slightly to the now hysterical motorists lined up for blocks and drove away.

I smiled with a special satisfaction.

That couple has been married for fifty years, and I had just seen one of the reasons.

Whatever happened to the harmony?

a dELicAte

BaLaNce

# TWO FOR TEA

We cannot balance love
Like teacups,
For there are times
When love overflows,
Times the cup is
Less than full
And times when
Even our reheating
Does not warm
The cold, cold cup.

# SOMETIMES THE MUSIC DOESN'T STOP, IT JUST GETS VERY FAINT

Peter and Francie were not exactly a marriage made in heaven, but they both had a passion for skiing and the outdoors, and maybe somewhere in the cold country, despite Francie's constant complaints, they managed to keep their marriage frozen in place.

It wasn't that Peter was so terrible, it was simply that Francie was a perfectionist. She hated the way he gnashed his teeth, parted his hair and snored, and she made no secret of her opinion. "Peter," Francie would say loudly across a dinner table of sixteen friends, "why do you wear those ugly big glasses when you have a little face?"

Or, in front of his business associates, she'd ask sweetly, "Don't you hate that jacket on Peter? I do."

Of course you know what happened next.

One day Peter looked up from his desk at exactly the same moment as the young woman who'd just joined the firm.

And somehow, despite the fact that she was quite young and had good ears and eyes, she didn't hear the gnashing of his teeth or see the big glasses or the bad jacket.

What she saw was a very nice man, and these days nice men, no matter the color of their jackets, are difficult to find. So in no time at all, she let him know that he was appreciated. Really appreciated.

Did Francie find out?

Of course.

And when Francie found out, she jumped up and down and screamed and shrieked and threatened everything from calumny to self-destruction.

Peter, abashed and embarrassed, did not do what many men do. He didn't simply turn his back and wheel his life in new directions. No, he decided to stick to the old slopes.

It was difficult, but he did it. He bade goodbye to the lovely lady who'd become his lovely friend.

She left the office to seek another job (if you've noticed, in

these cases it's always the woman who finds she must leave), and Peter went back to what he hoped would be his happy home.

But Francie was suspicious.

Had Peter really given up that woman?

She had to know, so Francie started calling Peter six or seven times a day, some of those times when he was in meetings with others and had to be interrupted by a hand-delivered note saying, "Your wife is on the phone and says it's urgent."

Each time he took the call Francie said the same thing: "Are you sure she's out of the office?"

To prove his renewed fidelity, Peter started going home early from the office. He'd sit in the big chair in front of the window and read, and when he went in to have dinner with Francie, she'd greet him with stony silence.

And so she treated his return to the fold with unwanted calls during the day and unwanted silence at home.

Friends watched and said nothing.

All the friends, that is, except Joanne.

Joanne took Francie out to lunch one day and asked, "Why are you punishing Peter for returning?"

"I don't know what you're talking about," Francie said defensively.

"Of course you do," Joanne answered. "Peter did exactly what you wanted, and now you are not going to speak to him. You are going to make him eat humble pie for the rest of his life. How long do you think he will stand for it?

"Let me tell you a story," she said. "My first husband had a

number of oh, shall we say, indiscretions, and I pretended they never happened. Then one day I met a man who captured my heart and was kind to me. And so, even though I was married, I became involved. My husband found out and flew into a rage.

"Maybe all I ever wanted was to get my husband's attention. I'm not sure, but I quickly ended the affair and went home to be a faithful wife forever more. But he wouldn't let me do that. Instead he reminded me each day that I had broken our marriage vows. Never mind what he had done so many times. We

never referred to that. Instead I heard each day of my indiscretion, and then one day I woke up and realized that he intended to use this one mistake as a weapon over me for the rest of our marriage. That was the moment I packed my clothes, called my lawyer, and I was gone before he came home.

"You see, Francie," she explained, "my husband could handle infidelity; it was faithfulness he chose to punish."

No one yet knows whether Francie will listen to Joanne and relent. On paper it's easy to see that Joanne's advice is perfect, but sometimes it's not easy to take the advice that will save our lives.

# TROUBLED WATERS

My friend was in trouble.

I suspected it when we spoke on the phone and made a luncheon date, and I was sure of it when I slipped into the chair opposite her in the restaurant a few days later.

She held herself in that tight, don't-touch-me way that always says, "If you get too close, I'll break."

Of course, I had an idea what was bothering her.

The problem was a man.

Or, as we say, so what else is new?

Well, what was new is the oldest story in the world. She is young and good-looking and moving ahead in an important career. He is older and good-looking and already ahead in an important career. So far so good.

Now for the bad part.

She is unmarried. He is married.

Of course, he told her that he hadn't been really married for ten years—not part of a loving relationship like theirs, which was what marriage really is meant to be—and he said he'd always been waiting for a woman like her and besides, his wife ... oh well, you can probably write the rest of the story.

What none of us can write, however, is a happy ending to stories like this.

I tried to be comforting. I went through all those old bromides. I said she was better off without him. I said he was unfair to her and his wife. I said someday she'd be able to laugh. And all the time I talked, I knew she ached for him.

We lunched without eating, then kissed warmly and parted. And as I walked back to the office, I knew what I should have told my friend. . . .

I should have told her that she is Everywoman, because no matter how smart we are, each of us does foolish things.

I should have told her that the heart never asks the right questions.

I should have told her that the problem is that these things always start out innocently enough, but on our way to finding love, we lose our innocence.

I should have told her that one reason that these kinds of relationships are shining with stardust is that both lovers take time to enjoy the reality of the unreality. There are no stopped sinks in an affair.

And I should have repeated some other lines I had written in the long ago. . . .

I wish you knew what to do,
But how does a woman know when
She wants to change her life
And upset a clutch of people
In order to make herself happy?

When do you decide
You have the right to decide?

More important...
When does he?

Touching, isn't it, that in the world of the bomb and the boom and the bust, women still cry over the men they shouldn't.

# A LITTLE
# NIGHT MUSIC

I t was one of those nights you wouldn't want to miss. The company was as excellent as the food, and the house was really a home, a warm and loving home. As dessert was served, the hostess stood and raised her glass. "Tonight I salute John," she said. "I have saluted him many times in our marriage—but tonight I salute him with special love because this is our anniversary."

None of the guests had known beforehand, and so it was with genuine delight and surprise that we toasted the couple in love and friendship.

For this indeed was a marriage of love and friendship, a long-running marriage. Forty-eight years, to be exact.

There were some good-natured laughs and jibes, and as I sat there I thought about this precious marriage.

What makes a marriage stay a marriage?

I asked John, the long-ago groom. "It takes a loose rein to keep a marriage tight," he opined.

Isabelle, his wife, was more prosaic: "We expected it to work."

But there is yet another question I have considered for some time. I finally asked John, "Although you have been married to Isabelle for forty-eight years, how many wives have you had?"

He thought for a moment. "Four or five. No, six or seven. The point is," he said, "Isabelle has changed a great deal. What I married was a girl with blue eyes. What she has become is a very competent woman with a number of interests and talents. And I have changed to keep up with her. I have also changed to keep up with myself. We are neither of us the person we married."

Changing and becoming.

Isn't that what most of life is about?

Yet some things do not change.

And as I looked at John and Isabelle I knew that what never changed for them were the feelings, the commitment that they made and kept.

Only the style was different.

# THE SIX-ACRE
# HUSBAND

*I* love to read the Sunday magazine real estate ads, the ones with pictures.

I get a kick out of looking at houses I'll never live in and driving my dreams up sweeping driveways, reading under beamed ceilings and creating perfect soufflés in captivating kitchens (although the kitchens are obviously intended not for owners, but only for maids and caterers).

These ads are my Sunday funnies, all part of what I call my weekend fantasy life.

At least they were until I came across that ad.

It was an ad for a house that looked like the kind you'd see in a TV miniseries, assuming you were watching a story about the very oiled and somewhat spoiled in Miami.

But what really set this house on the water in Florida apart from the others was the price. Or rather the nonprice.

The headline, instead of giving the location or some compelling selling fact, said simply, FOR SALE/TRADE.

And the copy went on to say, "Magnificent California contemporary 6 BR 7½ BATH. 8,000 sq. ft. living."

From there it went to all the other goodies the house had, the pool and spa, the display area for cars, gourmet kitchen and blah blah blah.

But it was the last line of the ad that really got to me. Instead of a price tag the deal was, "Would consider trade up or down for Upper East Side Manhattan apt. or house, jet/turbo/aircraft/ yacht."

I put the paper down slowly.

Somehow the real estate ads didn't seem like so much fun today.

What was this all about?

Home is where the jet is?

Has the no-class society evolved into the no-price home?

I wondered who on earth would ever place an ad like that.

Later that day, around six o'clock, I walked past the church on our corner. There was a line of homeless queued up for their Sunday night meal, just as I have seen them for a couple of years now.

I looked at faces where hope had faded and despair had taken over.

As I continued walking, the two pictures juxtaposed in my mind—the Sunday picture house of the over-homed and the Sunday night line of the no-homed—and I thought that there finally comes a time when too much is not enough. Too much money does not buy values. It does not buy reality, and it does not help one sleep at night.

In this hungry, homeless world, who would place an ad like that?

Which person I see striding down the avenue every morning, which of the people scrambling for position in our two-tiered society, the comfortable haves who step over the have-nots on their upwardly mobile way, would write such an ad?

I asked myself as I walked uptown to a party that night, a simple little party with friends, and there was a wife I knew. She and her husband had separated in recent days, and it was one of those messy kinds of separations caused by his very public fling with another lady.

"I suppose you've heard," she said.

I nodded.

She shrugged her shoulders. "I loved him. I really did," she said. "There he was, the best in his profession and the two of us with houses, cars, travel, a fantastic life. He had it all—but he wanted more."

I heard a buzzer beep in my head.

Now I knew who could place an ad like that.

Wasn't her husband the kind of man who would trade the picture for the dream?

Goodbye house, so long wife, and hello jet/turbo/aircraft/yacht...with matching girlfriend. Trade the house and toss in the wife.

The trading season isn't confined to sports teams, and every business has its bonus babies. Even the wife business.

Did this wife/husband story have a happy ending?

Depends who's telling the story.

He suffered a series of business reverses, and the lady who was so anxious to marry him drifted off to another title on a bigger door.

Who ended up with the errant husband?

The wife who waited.

She wasn't kidding when she said she really loved him, and she proved once again that sometimes you have to play the waiting game to win the mating game.

# THE DOLLAR-A-YEAR MAN

To live with one man
All one's life
Is the ultimate dream;
But show me one man
Who ever stayed one man.

For men,
Like women,
Add, divide and multiply
Many times
In one life.

So even though we
May balance budgets,
We all have difficulty
Juggling the small change.

# THE CHARITY
# DANCE

ig charity parties all tend to look alike after a while—and this one was no different.

In the candlelit ballroom of the hotel, some couples were dancing to a famous orchestra, others were looking at watches and wondering if it was too early or too late—too early to leave or too late to expect a good time.

And then we saw Tom.

No hello.

No how-are-you.

None of the "old pal, hi, great to see you" greetings we always expect from Tom.

Instead Tom said grimly, "I suppose you heard."

"What?" I asked.

"I resigned this morning. They sold the company, and I'm not working for *those* guys. Best thing I ever did. It'll be great."

And then Tom turned around to stop another friend. "I resigned . . . it'll be great," we heard as we walked slowly on.

"I hope he's right," my husband said. "I want him to be able to do what he wants."

I agreed. Tom is one of those grown-up teddy bears with enthusiasm for life and affection for friends. But he is also a high-powered executive whose life has been limousine-lined, gold credit–carded and first-class traveled.

I said nothing, but I wondered how Tom would do in the back of the plane.

My husband did articulate it, however. "Tom's life won't be

the same. And Mary's life won't be the same either."

No indeed.

Tom will have to live a new way, and Mary will have to carry his new baggage.

How will Mary do? I wondered.

What most of us forget in this, the years of the mega-mergers and super-buyouts and re-formed corporations and dying industries, is that under the fancy figures are small, human figures.

It's not easy to take a man from his job at any time. I guess that's because men, much more than women, tend to identify themselves not by the company they keep but rather by the companies that keep them.

Every man is a few people, and what he claims to be during the workday identifies him and determines his behavior and lifestyle after he leaves the office.

But now jobs are being lost, shuffled, redealt. And so are identities.

Life is becoming less what we make it and more what bankers and stockbrokers make it.

And in this world of redefined men, there will be a lot of women who will feel powerless and out of it.

We will all try to be nurturers, but we'll all learn that it is a lot easier to encourage him when he's working.

We'll try to be a support team, but we'll all see that we are often refused, rebuffed and rejected.

We'll try to say, "It doesn't matter what you do. It will work out; it will be good."

In some lucky cases we'll be right.

But in all cases we'll try.

For no matter where the stock goes or when the job comes,

no matter how keenly we feel his disappointment, regardless of the downs in his life, we will be there with all the encouraging words because a good love doesn't quit even when a husband does.

# FAME IS A
# FOUR-LETTER WORD

She was famous for being famous, a woman whose name was a fashion, whose predilections were precursors of style.

If hemlines went up, hers were upper.

When a remote island became the next place to play, it was because she'd already anointed the beach with her suntan oil.

She ran off with a rock star one season, someone else's husband the next.

But marriage was not on her menu. "Tryst, not trust," was her credo. And in the hell-bent-for-fun days, that seemed a satisfactory slogan for girls with more dollars than love.

However, with the first news of AIDS, she sensed that safe sex and commitment would become the fashion. So she married the man of the moment, an up-and-coming stockbroker. And from the day they married, it seemed that all over the world marriage became the thing to do.

But marriage, like the island that in time was populated with all the wrong people, attracted the wrong people, too. Well, there was really just one wrong people.

Him.

Marriage was just not big enough for both of them.

So she did what any sensible woman would do. She ended the marriage and took up with a man a rung higher on the fame ladder. He was famous for the starlets he discovered and the designer drugs he used. She didn't have much use for the nymphet starlets she met through him, but she rather liked the drugs to which she was introduced.

She liked the drugs so much that by the time they celebrated their first anniversary, she couldn't remember if it was their first month, their first year or their first century.

By the second anniversary—second year—he had skipped with one hundred pounds of nymphet and a ton of her money.

That was when she went into analysis.

Can't sleep, she complained.

Any problems? the doctor asked.

No, none, she told him.

The doctor looked closely. Are you on drugs? he asked.

She shook her head.

But the doctor prescribed nothing. He knew she didn't need more pills.

She came to the doctor each day, lay on the couch and told of her past. She told about the men and the parties and the good times.

Carefully he tried to bring her to the present.

Carefully she avoided the present.

The doctor looked for her name in the columns. Ordinarily he didn't read gossip, but he wanted to relate to her world with her. He brought up the names he saw in fresh type.

They weren't in her cast of characters.

The doctor nodded. So that was part of her unhappiness. She was already out of date. She had outlived the freshness label on her life.

The doctor suggested that she go to a famous clinic. Even doctors know that famous people will consider only famous clinics.

She frowned. Isn't that for druggies?

Yes, he told her. That's why you ought to go there.

I'm not on drugs, she insisted.

Go anyway, the doctor urged. Your name will be in the papers if you do.

She laughed. Let's get married, she suggested.

I have a wife, he told her.

Then give me some pills.

If you need some, you'll get them at the clinic, he promised.

When she came back from the clinic, she went on the lecture circuit and told all. She was a feature story in four magazines, did six talk shows and was happy for three months. But the talk shows didn't rebook her, and by the time the magazines were old enough to be recycled, she was in need of a little recycling, too.

She went back to the doctor.

The clinic didn't work for me, she explained.

But you got off the stuff, he reminded her.

Did I? she asked.

You're still young and beautiful, he assured her.

Then why aren't I famous? she asked.

You have to be famous for something, he explained. Look, you were just famous for being an example of a woman who can get off drugs and make life worth living.

Why is life worth living? she asked. Who loves me?

Do you love someone? he asked.

I get love, she told him coldly. If you're famous, you don't have to give it.

The doctor started to correct her, then reconsidered. Even an analyst has trouble telling a proud woman she is no longer famous.

When she took the overdose, her name appeared in print for the first time in seven months.

She rated a mention on the front page plus a full-column obituary and a picture.

Since that day it's been almost impossible not to find her name in the papers.

Two writers are doing books about her.

Three networks are vying for the miniseries.

The doctor reads each item ruefully.

If the lady were alive, she wouldn't need him at all.

She's finally famous on her own.

# OF LIFE
# AND LOVE

Small lives are so
Because they have small goals;
Small loves are so
Because they have small hopes.

# A HALF-TURN
# TO THE LEFT

From the back Linda could fool the world.

Put her on a bar stool, give her a half-turn to the left, and you'd swear that you were looking at the body of a well-built nineteen-year-old.

It wasn't until the lights went up that you could see the little frown lines around the mouth and the first gray hairs that came with the territory at thirty-nine. Still, Linda was a dish, and she moved as if she knew it.

Maybe it was her insouciance. Maybe it was that long, sensuous line of her back. Whatever it was, it made Linda the first thing Don saw when he came into the bar and grill. He looked and smiled with appreciation, but then—then he looked and smiled with a vague recognition.

No, it was just the dim lights, wasn't it? Or was it—?

No, couldn't be. She'd be an older woman by now. But there was something about the way this girl held herself that was so familiar, so much like—forget it.

And then, just as he was about to catch a seat at the bar, the girl on the bar stool spun a half-turn to the left.

Wow!

It was—

It was Linda!

Don didn't even remember rushing to her and embracing her. All he could remember was holding her close and murmuring,

"Linda, oh Linda." His face and arms were full once again of that sweet smell and feel.

"You're still a White Linen girl?" he teased.

"Mmmmm," she mumbled. Who but Don would know the name of her fragrance at a moment like this?

"Whatever became of us, Linda? What happened?"

She threw her head back and laughed. Now he saw the lines that came with the years.

"What happened, Don? You happened. You happened to find my best friend more interesting than me."

"Oh, right. Right. What was her name?"

"Anne," she lied.

"Anne? That doesn't sound familiar."

"It shouldn't. It wasn't her name, but I figured that somewhere in that hotshot macho world of yours, there must have been an Anne."

"You're still at it, aren't you? Still got that smart, tough mouth?"

"Get off my case, Don. It's been too many years." She started to push back from the stool.

"Wait," he cried impulsively, "don't leave me again. This time give me a chance."

She stopped. "A chance?"

"Please," he begged.

A chance? No one had asked for a chance for three years, not since she and Billy had been divorced. She thought of the empty nights and the empty guys. She thought about the peanut butter sandwiches she ate standing at the kitchen sink. And she thought what fun it would be to cook for a man, kiss a man, go to the movies with a man. If she said no, she knew what would happen... nothing. But if she said yes—and if this time—

Well, what did she have to lose? At least this would be a boyfriend who came fully equipped with mileage and history. Better than looking for some dude who'd only disappoint her on a new level. Maybe it was time for a summer rerun.

"You've got it, Don. I'm giving you a chance."

Don went home with Linda that night, and he didn't leave the next morning, the next week or the next month.

Over the summer they reviewed and retold their love story, which they titled Chapter Two, to anyone who would listen.

They would tell how they'd met twenty years earlier at college, dated, fallen in love, and then they would reenact the moment Don walked into the bar and Linda took that half-turn to the left.

The question their friends would inevitably ask was, "What happened twenty years ago?"

Don had the answer. "Her father didn't approve," he would answer chastely.

"Why would he?" Linda would ask lightly. "Who'd want a daughter to go out with the captain of the stag line?"

Everyone would laugh a lot at that. Linda was a real pistol.

The first time Don struck her, Linda rocked back in surprise even though she knew she'd deserved it. Make too little, spend too much: that had always been her problem. She'd felt bad about his hitting her, but she didn't blame him. Not that time.

The next time she knew that she had really asked for it, dared him to hit her. That time it was about money, too. She'd bought six boxes of raspberries. "Who do you think you are? Mrs. Getty?" he'd snarled.

After that she was more careful, and he cooled down, but Linda noticed something new about herself: she was getting absentminded. Is this what love was supposed to do to you? "I think I've got early Alzheimer's," she told Rebecca, who worked with her at the hospital.

"What makes you say that?" Rebecca inquired indulgently.

"I can't find my pearls," Linda confessed.

"Hey, the stores are full of them."

"But these are ones my parents brought me from Japan."

The next thing to be mislaid was her diamond stud earrings, then her watch. Finally when her wallet was counted among the missing, Linda got a really bad feeling in the pit of her stomach.

Don wasn't angry when she asked him about it; instead he sat down and had a long talk with her. He told her he was really disappointed in her, he'd thought their love was above suspicion. And he told her that he didn't want her to worry. If they found that she really had a mental problem, he'd be there at her side.

Then he left to go to work at the sporting goods store.

That was the night she found her empty wallet in his closet along with boxes of unopened golf balls and tennis balls, all with labels from the store where he worked. Linda shut the door and leaned against it.

So she wasn't losing her mind.

But she could.

If she stayed, she'd lose her mind, her money, her sense of self.

Linda walked to the bedroom, looked around this place where the love had burned so bright despite these dark undercurrents. She packed her clothes, paused at the door, thought for a moment, then walked back in and pulled out a piece of paper and a pen, wrote a quick note and pinned it to her pillow. "Dear Don," it read, "Next time I'll take a half-turn to the right."

# SMALL-TOWN GIRL

She was a small-town girl who divorced back in the days when divorce was a big-city thing to do. So she did what small-town girls did in those days: she moved to the big city.

It was the right move.

She found people she liked and places she liked, and before long she went to a party and even found a man she liked. Funny thing was that although they met in the big city, he was from a teeny town.

Turns out that the teeny-town man liked the small-town girl, and by the time they were this far in the story, they were a couple.

The longer our small-town girl stayed in the city, the more the city clung to her. There were little cinders of sophistication in her walk, and, as a result of constant theater- and concert-going, her talk was sprinkled with two scoops of Shakespeare and a dollop of chamber music.

But the city had the opposite effect on him, and the more he put on black tie, the more he yearned for no tie at all. There were nights when he walked along the city streets and could swear that somewhere in the back of his head a coyote was howling.

So despite their growing affection, in spite of a couple of years of closeness and sweetness, he faced her with his news: he couldn't take the city. Not really. He knew she loved her friends and her life, but it wasn't for him. He didn't like a steady diet of parties, and champagne and truffles just made him hungry for pie and coffee. With a heavy heart, he picked up and

moseyed back to his teeny tiny town.

She was sad and lonely at first, and little by little she began to pencil new names in the date book, and somehow she kept running. Once in a while she'd look back and think how nice it would be if the man on her arm were the man she really wanted on her arm—

And down in the horse country that he loved, he'd look at the other rocking chair on the front porch and think about the girl he wished was a-sittin' and a-rockin' with him.

Then one day the phone in his one-room cabin jangled, and it was his big-city lady. "I miss you," she said.

"I miss you," he said.

And by the time the conversation had ended, he'd made his plans to come to visit her.

He stayed for two weeks, and it was the best of times.

When he went back, he called and told her to come on down.

She kept explaining that she just wasn't meant for teeny places, but he got her when he said, "I went up there for you—"

So, with high resolve, she got on the plane and went to visit him. I will not say I don't like it, she promised herself. I'm going to try to like it. I like him. Why wouldn't I like his life?

He was waiting when she got off the plane, and they got in his terrific four-wheel drive and headed for the farm.

She closed her eyes, silently repeated all her promises to love his life, opened her eyes, found herself in his cabin and immediately burst into tears. "I can't do it," she sobbed. "Send me home."

Back she went to the big city.

But no sooner was she back than she missed him once more.

And no sooner had she left than he wanted her.

"What will we do?" she cried on the phone one night.

"I've got the answer," he promised. "I'll come to see you in the summer, and we'll go up to the country. We can play golf and sit and rock on a porch. Then I'll go back to my teeny tiny town and you can go back to your big city."

And so they do meet now every six weeks or so.

"It's better than some marriages," he says.

"And it works better than divorce," she says.

"I love him," she explains, "but I can't live someplace where I'm the only thing in town that's happening."

"I love her," he explains, "but I can't live where everything that happens goes on outside my house."

"It's Same Time, Next Year," is her comment.

"More like Same Time, Next Month," he adds.

And what does this prove?

Simply that an improvisational relationship can sometimes be more lasting than a formal one. And even a little love works better than no love at all.

# DIVORCE
# ADVERTISING STYLE

The model in the ad had a pouty little mouth, and her body was wrapped in fur and curved toward the camera in that come-to-me look.

But it wasn't the picture that stopped me.

It was the headline of the ad. It read, THE "DIVORCE IS FINAL" COAT.

And the copy read, "O.K. So it didn't work out. The important thing to remember is that there are lots of other people out there who have gone through the very same thing. And also remember that there are lots of people out there to fall in love with again. Well...maybe not lots. But certainly one or two." There were a few more platitudes, and then came the words, "So you lost the man of your dreams. Find the fur of your dreams at——"

I tried to read the rest of that ad, but I was so mad my glasses were steaming.

I put the paper down.

Who would dare to tell you that a fox in the picture could replace a man who was no longer in the picture?

That was written by a man, I thought. Or else it was written by a woman who doesn't know the first thing about divorce.

For starters, most of us learn that divorce isn't the beginning of the dream of the fur coat; it's the end.

It is also the end of the dream of the new washer and the frequent baby-sitter. Divorce doesn't leave most women with more money—it leaves us with less expendable income. It is men who find that their standard of living goes up when they go out.

But it isn't the money part of that ad's philosophy that bugs me; it's the flip attitude toward divorce.

It is that attitude that says divorce is just another little adorable adventure, a giggle with the girls, another one of those buy-and-sell occasions, and so long as you buy something to mark the occasion, everything will be okay.

But most of us know that you can't buy anything to hide the big hurts of life.

For most of us, divorce is more than a small bump on the road of life.

Divorce is a kind of widowhood that can leave a woman even more isolated than death, because divorce is in our hands and death isn't, and some people don't trust those who take life's events in their own hands.

Sometimes divorcing couples learn that they have been the glue that held a lot of other marriages together—even as theirs was crumbling.

But, most important of all, most women take their marriage vows seriously. We were all raised on the same goody-goody movies and happy-ending books. We all wanted to be part of the perfect television family.

We wanted love and comfort and a man who listened. And we wanted that man to be our husband–lover–best friend.

But for some of us, no matter how it began, it didn't get better.

And sometimes when things don't get better the way they are, they need to be changed.

But a fur coat—before or after the divorce—won't be the answer to our dreams. New coats won't keep us in old, worn-out marriages.

And new coats won't warm us when our hearts grow cold.

No matter what advertising copywriters try to teach us, most of us already know that there are some things in life you can't buy.

# COME FLY
# WITH ME

I f you measured people the way you do property, you could say that Shari measured fifty by ninety—a fifties-type mentality in a nineties-style body.

Shari was superbeautiful, very smart and medium talented. Teddy was two inches shorter than his wife and considerably shorter on looks, brains and talent. But, in true fifties tradition, Shari was just wild about Teddy.

If he voted the straight Republican ticket, so did she. If he switched to the Democrats the following election, so did she.

She darned his socks and damned his family—but did neither in public. She was, by all accounts, the perfect and proper wife, who cooked everything from health foods to rich cassoulets.

So what was wrong with the marriage?

Just one thing.

Shari did not participate in Teddy's passion for biplanes.

Teddy spent all his weekends at the local airport, where he took apart, put together and flew biplanes.

Biplanes?

It took three Dramamines, six friends and a long talk to get Shari on a jet. Shari was the kind of woman who got airsick just driving to the airport.

At first Teddy thought it was adorable the way Shari resisted sharing his interest. He treated her fear of flying as an endearing quirk in their otherwise perfect relationship.

And then one day Shari went to pick up Teddy at the hangar where he worked on his biplanes, and there was a very pretty woman in overalls looking adoringly at Teddy while he explained the working of biplanes.

The next week Shari started flying lessons. She began with biplanes, moved up fast and soon soloed—in a jet.

Six months later Shari suggested to Teddy that they both give up their jobs and start a corporate jet service for companies that needed planes for a day or a week.

"You don't hate flying now, do you?" he asked with a smile.

"No," she answered. In truth she didn't hate flying. Not now. She'd hated it only when she didn't have control of the plane.

The business prospered, and executives renting the planes thought it was pretty cute to introduce their passengers to the captain, particularly after they'd asked her for coffee, tea or milk, the first assumption being that the pretty blonde was the stewardess.

It was two years later that the marriage ended, but it wasn't Shari's doing.

Teddy took a walk.

It seems he'd found a woman who looked like a stewardess and was a stewardess—and Teddy learned that the only thing that could make him happy was a woman who looked like a nineties woman but lived like a fifties woman. This stewardess was happy to keep both feet on the ground.

Not Shari.

Her life had changed, and she wasn't going back to socks and in-laws. So she started her own charter service.

And one day while flying a few big-time executives to a small meeting, she started a conversation—and now she's involved romantically with a corporate star.

"So what will happen this time?" her best friend asked.

Shari thought for a minute. "You know, all those years that I had a fear of flying—well, it wasn't really flying that scared me. It was love. I was afraid to make a really big commitment like turning my life into his. Then I did. I overcame fright for love. And the strange thing is that *my* love couldn't hold him. It was only *his* love that held him in place. So long as he could love what he did and who he was without competition, it was okay. But when I was at his side, he couldn't love me.

"So what will happen this time? I don't know. You see, I'm not afraid of love. But I don't know about this new man. Is he?"

# THE BEGINNING
# OF THE END

L ike all big things, it started with a small comment.

At a dinner party, I was seated next to our friend John, a very funny fellow who always gives the best toasts.

And why not?

John is successful in every part of his life. He adores his wife Patty, is a leader in his profession, in his community, and has the ability to hold lifelong friends and make new ones.

Just before John rose to toast our hostess, I whispered, "What funny thing will you say?"

He pushed his glasses back on his nose and turned to me with unaccustomed seriousness. "What I really want to say I won't. I'd like to say that it would be wonderful if we could all

stay as we are now, all feeling well, all doing well. But we know that in a year it won't be the same. It can't be."

John was right.

But what I never dreamed was that the biggest change would be for us.

How was I to know that within weeks the clock would stop ticking and the world would stop turning as my dear husband underwent major surgery?

How was I to imagine that with one diagnosis all priorities would change?

How could I have imagined myself a hospital zombie moving without thinking between home and hospital and concentrating only on his condition that minute, that hour, that day?

But it did happen.

It did happen, and we survived.

We survived the shock of knowing what was wrong, the pain of trying to correct what we were told could not be corrected and the difficulty in dealing with life after illness.

And, as we do from all of life's crises, we learned.

We learned that people can be very tender and caring in expressing concern. We were touched by the calls and letters, the flowers and plants, the books and balloons, the candy and fruit. However . . .

Some people called and asked for everything but the X rays in order to decide the seriousness of the situation for themselves.

Some people insisted on talking when we were beyond the ability to talk and listen.

Some people were so stunned by the news of Lee's illness

that they called me to weep long and loud, and I ended up reassuring them.

In this visual age where one picture is worth a thousand words, where television images assault us daily, where none of us—supposedly—has the ability to read, much less write, the greatest comfort for us both came in letters we received.

There were letters from people who see us regularly, people who had heard of Lee's illness and had not seen either of us for some time. But each person and each letter managed to give him and me a kind of strength that no other gift could.

When we knew that Lee had made it through the tough surgery and that life would go on another day or week or month, my husband turned to me and said, "You know what really matters? Your immediate family and close friends; the rest is Barnum and Bailey."

So together we made a decision and consciously turned our back on the circus.

In that long, sweet summer of our marriage we held each day close.

To a friend who sent a letter wishing him well, Lee wrote in return, "My guess is that after this surgery I'll live six months or I'll live forever. Frankly, I'd prefer the latter."

It was what I'd have preferred, too.

But it was not to be, and after a year it was watch and wait, wait and watch, as the most precious life in my life faded like an old daguerreotype that crumbled in my hands.

But I could still hear the music.

Still I sang his songs, and even now he never mentioned that I couldn't carry a tune.

One day I said to him, "I've never told you this, but you're the only person in my life who ever let me sing out loud. When I was in school, I stood in the front row and moved my lips because I threw everybody off. Everybody in the world agrees I can't carry a tune."

Lee took my hand and said, "What do they know? How can *they* hear you? Kid, you sing *my* songs."

# Remembered Melodies

# THE DAY
# THE MUSIC
# STOPPED

**D**eath was the thing we always joked about.

"If you die first, I'll kill you," he'd say.

"Don't die," I'd plead. "I'm too old to discuss my sun sign with strangers."

I guess we thought that if we laughed about it, we'd hold fast to life, stop time and the river.

We were wrong.

Extraordinary love does not get special long-life rewards.

But, oh, it was a special love.

We came to love each other after we'd scaled other heights and plumbed other depths. We were long past youth, but we had a very young love, a love that took pleasure in Saturday walks and Sunday papers, a love that worked in Africa and in Paris, and—best of all—a love that grew at home.

Homegrown love doesn't make headlines anymore.

But in the richness of our homegrown love, we had time to prepare for his death.

Still we were not ready. He was not ready to leave me, and I could not bear his going. So, although we had both time and opportunity, we never talked about death. We talked about life, and we made polka-dot plans for ways to celebrate our love. And when he spoke—in the beginning it was with paragraphs,

later it was with words, and in the end it was with his eyes—
the core of his being, the essence of his dignity was there.

I take comfort in those memories, just as I take comfort in
the outpouring of letters and telegrams and calls that came in
the days after he died.

Lee was a man of the theater, and our family heard from
directors and actors and managers, men and women who said
things like, "Lee gave me my first break," and "He wasn't afraid
to take a chance on a kid. I'll never forget what he did for me."

I'll never forget what he did for me as his wife either.

He made my half-focused dreams of love come sharply to life.
A man I know said not long ago, "You must be very happy in
this marriage. There's no heartbreak in your poetry anymore."

It was true.

I wrote of him and life's joys.

I wrote of him and triumphs of the spirit.

Now he is gone, but my poetry and my words will not go back
to the small, unhappy place where once they were.

I know that I will never be as isolated in my new grief as I
was in my old unhappiness.

Lee's legacy is priceless, for he gave me a view of life and
people, a sense of myself and my own worth as a loving woman.

He showed his children, his friends and me how a man must
live and how a man must die. He did both with a dignity and
grace that none of us will ever forget.

No, he didn't live long enough. But he did live long enough to
make an indelible impact on those who knew him and those

who knew him only through his work.

He left memories of love and tenderness and courage.

He left a good name.

He left, but he will never be gone to those of us who loved him passionately and will forever.

Isn't that a kind of immortality?

# RIDING ON EMPTY

When you were here
And each day throbbed with life and joy and you,
My heart was full.

But now that you are gone
And I no longer play the daily drama of our lives,
My heart is empty.

And, my love,
None but the empty heart knows
The heavy weight of life.

# AFTER WORDS

Sometimes I worry that I do not keep all of Lee alive, but reach instead only for those parts of him I need. I keep his smile.

I hold tight to his humor, his loving jibes. I've noticed that whenever I get too sure of me, I can hear, "Hey, Gonzo."

He still can cut me down without cutting me up.

But then I guess all of us who've lost someone—no matter the reason for the loss—all do what we need to do in order to put one foot before the other and march on with life.

A woman in Venice, Florida, told me that she'd decided to

stop wearing her wedding band, and so she took her band and his and had them melted into a gold nugget that she wears on a chain around her neck. "I finger it often," she admits.

I'm not surprised.

An Ontario widow admitted that it took her twelve years to cleanse the grief inside her. She also said that widowhood makes us all "no longer strangers but closer than sisters."

That's good. We need all the sisters we can get.

Seeing her husband through a long terminal illness caused another woman to say, "It was not an easy time. I was half dead and he was half alive."

Some widows are left with a mission.

A Kansas woman whose husband of twenty-two years was killed in Pan Am Flight 103 over Scotland is determined that her husband's death at the hands of terrorists will be remembered, so that others will not have to die, too. She has formed a group with other families of victims.

In Pennsylvania a woman admitted that when her desperately ill husband died, she didn't wish him back—not at first. But a year later, the memories of the last illness dimming, she confessed, "If I could just hold him again, tell him again how I love him and ask him for some advice."

A Florida widow is annoyed by people who avoid her because they don't know what to say. "Don't they understand," she asks, "that there isn't anything to say, and all I want is someone to have fun with?"

No, I think a lot of people fail to understand that most of us

want life after widowhood. We don't want to insult old memories, but we'd like to create some new ones.

No one was more perceptive in discussing her widowhood than the woman in North Dakota who was widowed thirty years ago, remarried, and has lived happily ever after. Life goes on. But the widow/wife said knowingly, "You'll never completely recover, and you'll never want to."

# THE ART
# OF LIVING

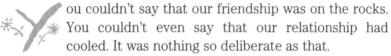

ou couldn't say that our friendship was on the rocks. You couldn't even say that our relationship had cooled. It was nothing so deliberate as that.

It was just that over the years Joan zigged when I zagged, and we were never in the same place at the same time.

But today we were.

Today, for reasons too dull to explain, we were seated face-to-face at the same luncheon, and we immediately started to play catch-up, to put ten years on the table, before the last lettuce leaf disappeared.

"Your husband—" she began.

My eyes filled.

"Your mother—" I answered.

Now *her* eyes filled, and with unspoken words each of us finished the other's thoughts.

How Joan must miss her artist mother, I thought, for the two had had a very special relationship, that kind of mother-and-daughter bonding that brings the generations closer but doesn't shut out the rest of the world.

I reached over and squeezed Joan's hand. "What are you doing now?" I asked.

I've found that to be a good question when I'm not quite sure what to say next. Deal with the here and now. Ask the easy questions, the easiest of which is, "What are you doing these days?"

She looked at me for a minute, and then she said, "I could tell you in two words, but first I want to tell you a story. It's so strange for me to tell you because it's kind of spiritual, and you know that I'm not a mystic. I don't talk to chairs, I never hear the wind whistle my name, and I don't even believe I'm going to a better world when I leave this one. Still, this did happen to me. Now with that preamble, do you want the two-word answer or the story?"

"The story," I assured her. "Yes, I want to hear the story."

And so she began...


"When my mother died, her house was left to me. It's a place that I love because it's filled with my happiest memories. It's where my mother did most of her painting and where she entertained so frequently.

"The first thing I did when I took over the house was to paint and paper and slipcover furniture. You know, I wanted to make my kinds of change, and so I did. In time I felt the house fit my psyche just as it had once molded to my mother's. But there was one room I didn't touch. I couldn't; it was Mother's studio, and I left it just as it was.

"I really didn't go into the studio at all, but I lived very happily in all the other parts of the house.

"And then one night, one ordinary stars-in-the-sky night, I went to sleep, and in my dreams my mother came to me.

"'Are you painting?' she asked.

"And I turned to my mother, and I said rather dispiritedly, 'I never was much good. You gave me all those lessons, but—'

"My mother just disregarded what I was saying; she interrupted me and said, 'Go to my studio tomorrow, and pick up the brushes.'

"'But I can't paint,' I protested.

"'That's all right,' she assured me. 'You hold the brush, and I'll paint.'

"When I woke up the next morning, I could scarcely wait to go to the studio. I opened the door, and sure enough, it was still just as my mother had left it. Her smock was on the hook. A fresh canvas was stretched on the easel. Even the rags were lying there.

"I walked to the place where the smock was hanging. I put it on and patted it over my body. And as I did, I sensed my mother's presence.

"I walked to the easel and picked up a brush. And then I put it in the oils. I dabbed here, touched there, stroked someplace else.

"Hours later—I don't even know what happened to the day—I stopped. I'd been painting all that time, but I didn't really know what I had painted. Now I decided to look. I wiped my hands slowly, almost afraid to see what was on the canvas. Then I stood back. I looked, and I gasped.

"On the canvas was a painting unlike anything I had ever done and infinitely better than anything I could produce. It was

not my mother's style, but it was not in the style of my earlier clumsy things either.

"I wiped my hands on the smock and walked slowly back into the house. I didn't tell anyone about my day because I wasn't ready to discuss or explain it. I needed time to think about it all.

"Two days later I went back to the studio, and there was this painting hanging there still, this painting that was too good to be mine. Yet it had to be. Still I said nothing.

"A week later I thought I'd look once more. Had I dreamed it or was it true that I had painted something that was new and different for me? I went back into the studio, and the painting was still there. But had this been a one-time phenomenon? I had to know, so I put on my mother's smock, patted it over my body, and immediately felt the sense of my mother. I stood at her easel, and once again I painted with a kind of style I'd never found by myself. It happens regularly now; I go to the studio, put on the smock, and my mother is there to guide me.

"Now back to your question," Joan said, smiling at me. "You asked what I'm doing these days. I said I could tell you in two words. Well, now that I've told you the long story, I'll give you the two-word answer to what I'm doing these days.

"I'm painting."

# DATING REVISITED,
## OR
# HOW I BECAME
# MY DAUGHTER'S
# DAUGHTER

I've traveled a lot in my life, but the strangest place I ever found myself was a no-man's-land—a real woman's world—called widowhood.

At an age when I thought the only new men in my life would be insurance salesmen, I found myself caught up in the improbable world of the suddenly single. In other words, I was dating.

That's how I happen to have assembled the case histories of an assortment of underdone men with overblown dreams. These newly anointed prizes include a collection of men over forty who would have interested very few females twenty years ago—but now, now with the statistics on their side, they suddenly find they are more sought after than a good maid. A man who can walk, talk, breathe and escort a woman all at the same time is today's number-one social prize.

I came to meet a number of these prizes because I listened to our friend Phyllis Cerf Wagner, who, when I predicted that I would spend my widowhood with women friends and work, told me in no uncertain terms, "You will not go into a women's ghetto. Of course you will see some women, but you'll also continue to see your friends, the couples you've known, and you'll find some nice men to take you out. You will not go out only with women or perennial bachelors who are always available as escorts. That's the easy way, easy for now, but it will ruin the rest of your life. Go when you're asked, and keep entertaining. When my husband [Bennett Cerf] died, I thought I must get out, and because I did I met Bob Wagner. We were both widowed, and we've had a divine marriage, a marriage of real, true, good friends. I'm not promising you'll meet any Bob Wagner, but whatever you meet is better than going out with women only."

So I did what I think is the hardest thing for a widow: I reestablished a social life. I began entertaining. I had small dinners at home and went to small dinners at the homes of friends. My life had been on hold, and now I was picking up old calls.

It was then that a friend, a magazine editor—let's call her Jane—rang up and said, "Lois, I have two men for you. One is a widower and one is a married man from London."

"A married man?" I asked, my voice edged with Shaker Heights shock.

"Oh yes," she said, "he's here often, and he'd like a little company."

"Look, Jane," I explained, "I'm not a candidate for the nunnery, but please, no married men."

"Just dinner," she added airily, "and we'll all be together. You, the two men, and my husband and me."

"Sure, sure," I answered.

The night of the dinner I did what I soon learned to do as second nature. I stood in front of my closet wondering if these men would be tall enough for me to wear heels. Or would they be the winners of the Toulouse-Lautrec look-alike contest?

The dinner went off pleasantly: the married man was more

interesting, but I never saw him again. The widower walked me home. He seemed nice enough and invited me to dinner the next week. We went to a screening, saw a man we both knew who did a double take when he saw us together and then said, "Oh, that's nice. That's good for you both."

I hated the man who said that. Don't ask me why. I don't know why I hated a lot of things people were saying. But what I hated most was those well-intentioned married persons who would pat my arm sympathetically and tell me, "You're lucky. At least you've known love." My standard answer was, "You're luckier. You still have love."

A few more dates with the widower, and I began to see some things I didn't like. He wanted—well, what's the difference, I stopped seeing him.

The next man was another widower who'd loved his wife. We had a mutual friend, and she arranged our meeting. It was very nice. He was a sweet, decent man. And I had absolutely no interest in him. He was like the kind of boy you meet when you're fourteen and your mother thinks he's really nice, and you can't stand him and you can't figure out the reason. That's how it was. A few weeks later he went to a party, met a widow, and she invited him to Wimbledon the next week. He went. But that gives you some idea of the kinds of temptations dangled before the eyes of these newfangled bachelors.

I'd still met no one who'd swept me off my feet, but it was getting kind of interesting to come home and see who was on my answering machine in addition to my daughter asking, "So how was this one, Mom?" One night there was a call from an old friend, and she'd heard about a terrific man, a widower who wanted to meet some women. She'd suggested me—although she hastened to add she'd never met the man herself, yet he did come with very good references.

He took me to a restaurant around the corner from my house, and he proceeded to tell me about the miracle woman who had been his wife—the smartest, the most beautiful, the best et cetera et cetera et cetera. I felt like Alice taking the shrinking pills: the more he talked, the more insignificant I felt. Finally he said, "Well, as my friends say, 'I've already had the Nobel Prize; from now on I'll just have to settle for the Pulitzer.'"

"Look," I said, "I've never even won a Pulitzer. Keep looking." Needless to say, he never called again.

I also went out with the Old Proper Rich Family Person, who spent every date telling me that his family was better than the families of all those men who were making all that filthy, terrible money. And then I finally did stop seeing him when he called to tell me how he could get a commission on all the trading done on my account if I'd just— I don't know what I had to do, all I knew was that I had to get him out of my life.

A very famous man was introduced to me at the home of equally famous people. He spent the whole evening telling me about the countess he'd just met. That's how I learned that there's nothing that can set you farther back in your social rehabilitation than meeting people who already know people a lot more interesting than you.

Another friend introduced me to a dentist, a widower. Three months after she gave him my name, he called. "Let's have a drink," he said. I called my friend, the name giver. "Look," I explained, "I'm out of a show-business marriage. I don't do auditions. What's this about? A drink. Then if he likes me, next time I get an appetizer?"

"No," the name giver explained, "he's a dentist. He doesn't have a lot of free time—"

I agreed; we had a drink. And he's one of the men I saw for a while. When I told him what I'd told our mutual friend, the name giver, about auditions, he told me that I was the sixth woman the name giver had sent him. He'd already *wasted*—his words —five dinners, and he wasn't about to be taken for a sixth.

Early on I realized that I was dating—dreary as it then seemed—because I had a few good friends who were willing to get involved. And it was one of those darling friends who reached out and hand-picked what turned out to be the right man for me. So, Dear Reader, if you're a happily married woman with a friend who's single for one reason or another, think about her. Call her. Invite her to your parties; introduce her to the extra man you know. The worst words a widow can hear are, "I know someone very nice, but I don't want to get involved—"

The world of the formerly married is full of women old enough to take care of themselves. Indeed that's all they have to take care of.

What single women don't have is enough love and friendship, and if old friends won't open new doors, who will?


# DON'T CRY, JESS

Jessica wasn't raised to be a widow.

She was raised to be a wife, and that's what she was for twenty-three good years.

She still remembers the day Cal said he didn't feel so good. It was his arm or his back— "Oh, well," she says now, "who can remember what the pain was? All I remember is that he was

hurting, and we went to the doctor, and from then on he wasn't the same. I don't mean he wasn't the same sweet guy. He just wasn't the same sweet *healthy* guy."

Now that he's gone—widows use a lot of euphemisms—she's searching for that one-of-a-kind inner strength she needs to keep her sorrow to herself. "I've read the grief and the self-help books, and I know you're supposed to get the sorrow out. But to tell you the truth, Cal wouldn't like that. He would want my sadness kept to myself. So now I find that work is the only thing that makes me sing. It's kind of like a pilot light, and it gives me a daily challenge to keep myself up. Cal would approve, I know that. You see, when he was sick he never asked the doctor or me, 'Will I die?' All he asked was, 'Will I live?'

"I suppose he got me ready for all this because he'd always told me about his father, who died when Cal was only eleven, and his mother had said to him, 'Lift up your head. Cry privately, not publicly.'

"Frankly I don't hold much to the theory of the stages of grief. I'm not mad, just overwhelmingly sad. I was cheated out of these good years. But hey, I had good years.

"Right now people like to rub up against me and make nice and pretend they're as sad as I am. I call them all The Energy Vampires, people who waste your time trying to make you unhappier than you are."

Jessica shook her head, and her eyes filled. "You know the worst time? It's four P.M. to seven P.M. each day. Those were the hours he'd come home—sometime in there I'd hear the screen door slam, and that kind of tentative, 'Jess, are you home?' He knew I was because the door was open, and when I'd ask him why he always came home with the same question, he was so damned sweet. He'd just pat my cheek and say, 'I can never

believe my luck.' And that was still going on after all those years.

"By the way," Jessica said with a rueful look, "I just named my car Sam. I figure a woman like me needs a man in her life. Now when people say in that sanctimonious way, 'Jessica, you really should get on with your life,' I smile and say, 'Sorry, I have to leave now. I'm going out with Sam.'"

# HEADS YOU LOSE, TAILS YOU LOSE

We were seated next to each other at dinner because of the law of supply and demand, an oversupply of women who dine with distinction and an unfilled demand for men with good table manners.

But that was all right with her and me. We belong to that liberated generation that prefers being cheek by jowl with one interesting woman than sandwiched between two dull men.

We ate around a few vegetables and poked at the veal before she mentioned her grown son, and I asked, "Are you married now?" That question proves we're contemporary women; a couple of generations ago one wouldn't quiz newly met persons.

"I'm a widow," she answered.

"Me, too."

"He was my second husband."

"Me, too."

"He died of a brain tumor."

"Mine, too."

"I was divorced the first time."

"Me, too."

Is it any wonder that less than a minute after we spoke I felt free enough to ask this woman I'd never before met, "Will you tell me which was more difficult—watching a marriage die as you did with your first husband or watching the man you love die?"

She folded her hands, looked down for a minute, and then raised her eyes and shrugged her shoulders.

"No contest.

"The worst is the death of the marriage. You see, when my husband was dying, I could *do* something. I could tend to his needs. Oh, he was irascible and made outrageous demands. At one point he insisted I call his office and get him two computers. But you see, I made the call. I could satisfy him even in dementia.

"It was my first husband I couldn't please, and it made me feel so helpless. I just stood there and watched the marriage being snuffed out, and there wasn't a thing I could do to light the fire, kindle the ashes.

"I think we women function so long as we can be useful, but there's no more useless feeling than a woman's when she watches a marriage end. I hurt more as a divorcée than I did as a widow; I was angry and unfulfilled.

"But my second husband, that darling young teddy bear of a man, died by inches loving me every step of the way. He left me rich."

# You Don't Have
## To
## Love Me Forever

It is not easy to be married;
It is not a simple thing
To be a part of someone else
When what I really want
Is to find the parts of me.

The diverse parts of me,
The funny sads,
The sad funnies;
I am changing all the time,
I can't keep up with me,
So I don't expect a love that knows no change;
I ask only that you
> Love me here,
> Love me now,
> Love me warm,
But you don't have to love me forever.

I mean that.

You don't have to love me forever;
But wouldn't it be something
If you did?

# THE WELL-
# DECORATED
# LOVE

Verna was half-past seventy when Franklin went to sleep, never to awaken again. It had been a full, rich marriage marked by the acquisition of those things that symbolize the marriage of success: multiple children, multiple houses, multiple charities and multiple honors—all secured within the parameters of the single marriage.

However, less than three months after Franklin died, Verna found that she was tired of sitting around and watching the division of the multiple assets. In short order she had wearied of the buys and the sells and the longs and the shorts. By October she'd had enough and was more than ready to abandon the lawyers and bankers and accountants who somehow appeared to make Franklin larger in death than he had been in life. He'd lived his seventy-eight years as a soft-spoken man of inherited wealth and culture, a man who guarded his privacy concerning money and investments. In death his assets, like a bag of uncut stones, clattered on the desktops of assorted money managers and rolled crazily about, and the greedy money men were ready to pluck at them for their own interests.

Most of the assets held little interest for Verna, but there was one that was—well, it was promising. It was a home in Florida, purchased more for Franklin and his golfing friends than for Verna. Still, she thought, the house might prove a suitable retreat for her and provide a project. Perhaps redecoration of the

house for her use and comfort might prove a symbolic way to say goodbye to Midwest memories and their shared life.

So, turning her back on the paperwork of death, Verna looked to life. In Florida she hired another widow, a sweet-faced interior designer, who guided her to the antiques shops catering to widows of wealth.

And that was how she met Swanton Lowe, a Southern gentleman who had taken to the antiques trade after years of genteel, middle-class office work in an uncle's paper mill. Swanton, alone now at age sixty-five, had been married once, a childless marriage of love that had ended when his wife died. Instead of remarrying, he had made a life of books and art and music, and now, at retirement, he'd found his life's best work, for in his role as antiques dealer he had the dollars to buy and sell things of beauty.

His widow customers were, he learned, all of a piece, the suddenly independently rich who had spent their lives as the dependent rich. Now, with their wealthy husbands enjoying their otherworldly reward, the earthly dollars had passed to the wives. Ladies who'd once needed permission to buy kitchen towels now found that they had the right to buy what they wanted without asking. The old ladies were wild with new power. Swanton clucked; someday when he retired he'd write his book and call it *A Widow's Pique.*

Verna bought several fine pieces from Swanton. He thought her different from the other sunshine widows, more thoughtful and subdued. He genuinely liked her Midwestern openness, her refusal to whisper, "Can't you do just a tad better on that price?" So, when Verna invited him to a dinner party for three other couples, including Verna's married daughter and her husband, Swanton accepted.

The day after the party Verna's daughter Cassandra called her mother. "What was that about, Mother?" she asked, her voice starched to a Midwest turn.

"What was what about?" Verna asked coyly.

Cassandra could barely speak, so outraged was she. "That young—man," she choked. "That young—"

"Young? My dear, he's old enough to be—"

"He's old enough to be a fortune hunter. Can't you see? He's making a fool of you. He's at least ten years too young for you. Look what he's doing. He sells you thousands of dollars' worth of junk—"

"It's not junk, Cassandra."

"I simply cannot believe this," Cassandra snapped.

"Try, dear. Otherwise you'll find that you're old before your time."

The next call was from Cassandra's daughter Melody. "Granny, how cute. I hear you're dating. What a flirt you are."

"Not really, dear."

"Go for it, Granny."

"Go for it?"

"I hear he's attractive, younger, and my mother is sure he wants your inheritance. Granny, I say that if he wants it, let him have it. Are you happy?"

"Yes. Yes, dear, I think so."

"Keep me posted, Gran."

A month later at lunch with her daughter and granddaughter, Verna let slip her secret. "I've been seeing a good deal of Swanton."

"Disgusting," Cassandra snarled.

"All ri-i-i-ight," Melody cheered.

"What can that man possibly see in you?" Cassandra asked.

"He loves antiques," Verna said softly.

Melody laughed.

"We're going to live together," Verna announced.

Cassandra gasped. "Not in the Midwest."

"Of course in the Midwest," Verna answered. "That's my home."

"But you can't, Mother. It's just not done. My father's been gone six months. What will everyone say if my mother *lives* with a man?"

"You're right, Cassandra," Verna admitted with an audible sigh. "It's just not the thing to do in the Midwest. So I guess we'll have to get married. Swanton wanted to get married, but I thought that would upset you. But I can see that living together would upset you even more."

Cassandra's mouth hung open in astonishment. Melody clapped her hands and kissed her grandma.

And so they were married, a year ago.

Then, just last month, Melody married her longtime college beau, and everyone agreed that the highlight of the wedding was the elegant granny and her dashing younger husband.

"Did he marry her for her money?" Melody's husband wondered.

"I hope so," Melody told him tartly. "Because if he did, that means there's none left for you and me. So you see, my dear groom, you'd better love me a lot because I may be all you're getting."

"I do, I do," he assured her. "In fact, the only other woman I could love this much is your grandmother. Honey, I figure she's what you'll be when you grow up, so I'll definitely stick around. I can't wait to live with you when you're Granny."

# WIDOW'S WEEDS

There are times when we say on paper the things we cannot say to one another. A woman wrote to me, "I lost my husband, too." Then she added a rueful aside, "Not true. We don't lose our husbands. They die."

"It isn't at parties or dinners that I miss my husband most," Nancy, a widow of two years, said. "What I miss is Tuesday night."

My friend Elga cleaned closets, desks and rooms after her husband died. She gave away most of his things to people who cared for him. "But I kept some jackets," she admitted. "I wear them a lot. Although they are old and don't quite fit me—well, they don't fit my body. But they fit me. You know what I mean."

# HELLO, LIFE

It was our wedding anniversary, the second anniversary after Lee's death, and I was pretending not to notice the day or month. I was working so hard at being new-normal that I even had a date and went to the theater.

As I stood with friends in the lobby and talked the typical dumb, standing-around talk, I reached to touch my ring. I know it sounds silly, but I never took my ring off after Lee died. I suppose I liked to keep touching the ring in order to assure myself that once there had been love.

Whatever the reason, I reached for the band and gasped.

The wedding ring, my beautiful sweet band of love, was broken. I could feel the broken part in my hand.

I was so stunned I told the people who were with me.

They nodded sympathetically and switched subjects.

It was smart of them because I didn't want to think about what it meant.

I did put the ring away for a while, and then I sent it to be repaired.

No one quite knows how the next part of the story came to be—but the ring was lost at the jeweler's.

The perfect jeweler who never lost anything lost my wedding band.

I was struck dumb by the news.

Did it mean Lee was releasing me—that he wanted to let me go and live the rest of my life?

I didn't know.

The man who had been with me that night asked me later if I thought the broken ring had meaning.

I shrugged and said to him what I said to myself: I don't know.

Then I told him—as I told every man who took me out—that I never wanted to get married again.

"Me, too," he sighed in relief, "but maybe this means we can see more of each other."

"Maybe," I said.

But what I really meant was that I would no longer feel that wherever I went, there were two of me.

For the first time I felt really alone.

It was scary, but it was life.

# Hello, Love

The broken ring didn't cause me to change my mind; I still didn't want to get married, but I did like going out.

As I think about it, I realize that the reason I liked going out was that it kept me from being alone. When I was alone I was forced to think back (oh, those painful memories) or look ahead (oh, that frightening future).

The present was all I could handle, and I thought I was handling it pretty well. My dating was kind of relaxed and friendly and noncommitting. At one point I settled into a regular dating pattern with one man, and that was okay. No whistles and bells, but who needs whistles and bells with eight grandchildren?

And then, the summer after my ring broke, Bud, who was an out-of-town widower, called. My friend Patty had given my name to her sister-in-law Cynthia, who, in turn, gave my name to Bud, who lived in her city. Patty (who refused to think I'd never marry) kept introducing me to new men as regularly as the postman delivers mail. I went out dutifully with each, and that just about sums up each of those dates—dutiful times but not beautiful times.

Meanwhile with the passing of the months I felt the tensions lessening in my body and mind as I went to work on a novel and found an escape route from real life through fiction. I wasn't yet ready to gamble on my life, but it was fun to play harmlessly on paper with other lives through characters I'd created.

It was at this time, a time when I was sniffing around the corners of life, that Cynnie's friend Bud called.

113

Bud wanted to come to town to take me out, and I agreed to see him. The problem was that we couldn't seem to find a date when we were both available.

Finally after a few calls and missed opportunities, we agreed on a date—for luncheon.

"Where do you like to eat?" Bud asked.

Immediately I was annoyed. If he's taking me to lunch, why ask where I want to go? If I pick an expensive place, I'm a gold digger. If I pick a so-so place, I have no taste. Then I had The Idea. I'd take him to a luncheon club atop an office building, a club where I belong, and no check would come to the table. It would be private, dignified—and if he turned out to be a twerp, I never had to see him again and I'd have taken him to lunch, so I played a courteous role for my friend Patty. But—oh, impossible but—if he were nice, I could say after lunch, "And now you owe me a luncheon."

Bud arrived first and tried to arrange to pay the check in advance. When he realized this private club didn't accept out-of-town privileges, he was embarrassed, and so—before he could even greet me in any fashion—he began his introduction with an apology at being my guest.

I relaxed. He might turn out to be boring, but at least he had manners.

We did all the usual introductory fillers—you know, the backgrounds (when and where we went to school, married, number of children, grandchildren and a few words about how we each came to know the women who'd introduced us). And then we got down to the personal pain. We'd both lost spouses to cancer. They'd both been diagnosed at about the same time. And they had died within days of one another.

"I've just started to go out," Bud said.

114

"But you've been widowed as long as I," I answered in surprise. "I started going out right away." I didn't tell him I went out because I couldn't stand thinking about my past or future.

"Going out?" he echoed in shock. "I can't understand how you could think about marriage so soon."

"Marriage?" I laughed. "Who said anything about marriage? I'm never getting married again."

He raised his eyebrows. "Why? If your marriage was as good as you say, why wouldn't you want marriage again?"

"Because—" I began, and then I said nothing. I couldn't tell him the real reason. I couldn't explain that I couldn't even think about marriage because I couldn't bear this kind of pain again. "Because—" I finished lamely.

He didn't pursue the subject. Instead he asked, "Do you know how I happened to call you?"

"Because Cynthia gave you my name."

"But that was a year ago," he told me. "I've known about you for a year. You see, Cynnie and Patty saw each other, and Patty asked her if she knew any suitable men for her friend Lois. When Cynnie told her about me, she also said that I'd been widowed, and Cynnie wasn't sure I was interested in going out. So Patty said that if he's a widower, he'd want to read a piece that Lois wrote in *Good Housekeeping* about her husband's death. Patty always carried the column with her, and she gave her copy to Cynnie. She told her to mail it to me. Well, I got a wonderful and warm letter from Cynnie with the column. I called to thank her and to tell her I wasn't yet interested in dating. I offered to return the column and letter, and she said, 'No, file it.' I was puzzled, and she said, 'Yes, file it under *AW* for *Available Widow*, and when you're ready, you'll know where to look.'

"I smiled about that, but when I decided to go out again, I looked in my drawer under *AW,* and there you were."

Somehow that story reduced the level of tension, and for the first time in a few years I—the *AW*—laughed without wondering why I was trying so hard to smile and laugh.

Lunch seemed only minutes from start to dessert. I don't remember what we ate, only that we talked more about our children (he had four; I had five) and grandchildren (we each had eight). We talked about people we both know and places we'd both been, and before I knew it, lunch was ended, and without even thinking that I had a preplanned answer should I like him, I said, really meaning the words, "And now you owe me a luncheon."

"All right," Bud said, "but I'd rather make it dinner."

We both operate with crowded schedules, so it took three months of time management to arrange that dinner.

But arrange it we did. Between our lunch and dinner, however, there were lots of telephone calls, lots of talking-together time and, by the time we saw one another again, lots of anticipated pleasure at being together.

No, I definitely did not want to get married again.

But, oh, I did want to see Bud again. . . .

# THE NEXT CHAPTER

And so we were married a year to the day after that first luncheon.

Bud proposed to me four months after we met, and

I asked for six weeks to think about us and the possibilities of a life together.

"Four months after meeting and you're thinking of marriage? That's pretty sudden, isn't it?" someone asked me.

Yes, it was pretty fast, but as I considered the possibilities during those six weeks I reflected on the fact that Bud and I were not exactly new to the love game.

Nor were we wild-eyed kids.

He had a life résumé. And so did I. He was not some unborn talent waiting to see the light of day. He had references and a history. So did I. Therefore, as I told the concerned person who was worried about the speed of our decision, what did we both have to learn that wasn't already in the record book?

Still, I knew that our marriage, any marriage, could pose problems.

I knew that Bud came from a marriage where he was the star, a marriage run on his schedule. I had been a part of a marriage of costars. We would have to adapt to sharing top billing and adjusting mutual schedules.

He's a man who loves the water and nature; I'm a city woman, thrilled by the theater and concerts and museums. So we would need to find ways to share our singular pleasures.

Still, I considered these things differences of style, not substance.

What would and could make our marriage work, I concluded, is our belief in God, family and responsibility.

He is passionate about the need to serve, to give back to the country and the world that have given so much to him.

I admire that.

It is easy at this time in life to pursue only personal pleasures, to seek beautiful people and handsome objects and never hear

the cries in the night. He not only hears the cries; he listens for them.

I don't think I could have thought about marrying a man who considered personal pleasure a way of life. Nor could I ever be content with someone whose sole pursuit is business and money. Balance, for me, is the most attractive thing about a grown-up man. And balance is evidenced by the way a man spends his time, apportioning his earned freedom to play with an awareness that the playground is not life's only arena.

So, as I considered the substance of the man, the fact that I found him bright and interesting (and that he found me so, too), I was almost ready to say yes.

Only one thing still held me back: the still-present fear of loss.

I talked to Bud about it at length. He was honest. He re-affirmed what I have always known: that although he may indeed love me very much, there was a limit to the promises he could make for our happiness. He does not come with a parts warranty.

What gave me the courage to say yes, in the end, was the realization that if we—all of us—are to live, we must accept the opportunities of life as well as the disappointments. I was becoming so good at unanticipated disappointment that I had almost forgotten how to treat unexpected joy.

I had forgotten my own dictum of a lifetime: *Nothing is forever. The good does not last, nor does the bad. Suffer the bad, for good will come eventually. Enjoy each moment of the good because it, too, will end.*

Maybe it was the timing that caught me off balance.

This whole romantic adventure did take over my life with amazing speed. It did happen at a time when I was still cozying

into a widow's shell, but, from the moment I met Bud, I knew in my heart that although the timing might be wrong, the man was right.

Finally I asked myself the last big question. What are you waiting for, Lois? Are you waiting until the timing is right and the man is wrong?

And so, when I said yes, I did it with all my heart.

With our children at our sides and Patty as matron of honor, we were married.

I rather like the feeling of newness that has come into my life at a time when I thought that everything I saw and did was a rerun of a fifties movie.

Now, despite my independent spirit, I find it comforting to know once again that where I am, when I get there and when I'll be home matters to someone. I like landing at an airport and having someone waiting at the other end to know I'm safe. And I like feeling safe in love.

So does Bud.

We've both had our share of tragedy.

Together we are determined to allow hope to triumph over history.

Together we are determined to enjoy learning the lyrics to yet another song of life.

P. S.

Happy

Anniversary

he best of marriages can know the worst of times, and similarly the worst marriages have their best moments.

Once I wrote a little book called *P.S. Happy Anniversary,* and dedicated it to friends who've gone on to many more happy anniversaries.

Because *P.S. Happy Anniversary* is about the good things we remember and the better things we anticipate—and, most of all, those things we appreciate—it seemed a fitting coda to these stories.

# P.S.
## Happy
## Anniversary

I was walking down the street today,
And suddenly I thought about you.

I didn't think about crossing with the light
Or which way the traffic moved
—or even if traffic moved—
I thought about you.

It was like a movie.
You know, when the film blurs
And they do
The Big Flashback.

Well, that's what happened.

The film blurred,
And there was a Big Flashback

—and I thought about you—

I thought about the way you were
The first time we met,
How you looked at me,
And I thought,

"If I hadn't looked that same look back at you,
Maybe we'd never have met,"

And just think what we would have missed!

We would have missed
A lot of long kisses,

A lot of short tempers
And all that wonderful making up.

We would have missed
Pretzels in bed
And watching the "Tonight Show" ... sort of ...
And the time you rolled over on the potato chip bag and said,
"What is this? A bed or a delicatessen?"

We would have missed
Tuition and camp fees and outgrown clothes,
Soft, wet kisses and very big hugs
—and somebody little saying, "I love you."

We would have missed
The first apartment with that terrible furniture,
The refrigerator door that opened into the hall
—and the joy of moving up and out.

We would have missed
Walking to work
322 bus rides
—and the pride in owning our first secondhand car.

We would have missed
Wondering how not to get pregnant,
Wondering how to get pregnant
—and the knowledge that we could do both.

We would have missed
The standee tickets,
The balcony seats
—and the thrill of moving up to the orchestra.

We would have missed
The goodbyes at airports,
The farewells at train stations
—and a lot of memorable hellos.

I suppose, my dear, that we have missed
The fun of giving and getting
Furs and jewels and trips to Hong Kong.
We have missed a castle in Spain, a villa in France
And sixty dozen opening nights.
But we haven't missed love,

Although there were times when it seemed so.

No, we haven't missed love.
Not too many couples can say that, I suppose.
Oh, we're busy with getting and gaining
And wondering where the stock is today,
But I know if the sky falls,
You'll come to me.